THE CHURCH OF JESUS CHRIST OF LATTER-DAY SAINTS

IN THE HAWAIIAN ISLANDS

by
Joseph H. Spurrier, Ed.D.
Professor of History
Brigham Young University
Hawaii Campus

PLUS

Selections from the
BOOK OF MORMON
in English and Hawaiian

ISBN 0-89036-114-2

Typesetting by

HAWKES PUBLISHING, INC.

3775 South 500 West
Salt Lake City, Utah 84115
P. O. Box 15711
Tel. (801)-262-5555

TABLE OF CONTENTS

Illustrations

INTRODUCTION

Most Americans and many others throughout the world are familiar with the contributions of The Church of Jesus Christ of Latter-day Saints (Mormons) on the mainland United States. From their history books they recall the young prophet Joseph Smith and his efforts to establish the restored Christian faith until he was martyred in 1844. Many remember the life of Brigham Young who led the world's largest mass migration to the desert area which has since blossomed into the state of Utah and other intermountain states. Still others are acquainted with Mormons because of the LDS temples which dot the globe or Church members who are prominent in business, education, entertainment, sports or who have served in government in countries throughout the world.

Equally as important, although not as well known, are the contributions made by The Church of Jesus Christ of Latter-day Saints in the Hawaiian Islands. As the third Christian religion to enter Hawaii following its discovery by Captain James Cook, the Mormons have worked with great diligence and sacrifice to teach the Hawaiian people since 1850. With the introduction of plantation laborers from Asia, the Mormons took their faith to the people of Japanese, Chinese, Korean, and Filipino background. Because of the unique needs of the people, the favorable political climate and the closeness to the principles of the U. S. Constitution as an American territory, Hawaii was selected as the location for the first Mormon temple built outside the continental United States. It was dedicated in 1919. Since that time, the Mormons have also established Brigham Young University/Hawaii, a major institution of higher learning, at Laie. Adjacent to the school as source of employment for its student body from throughout Polynesia and Asia is the Polynesian Cultural Center, a nonprofit educational institution.

As the LDS Church has reached out from its Utah headquarters to become an international organization, the Hawaiian Islands have taken on an increasingly important role in providing leadership and administrative skill in promulgating the principles of the restored gospel throughout the world. Since the end of World War II more than twenty mission presidents and their wives have been called to head missions in the Orient and other areas along with hundreds of other young missionaries who serve without pay. It is with a great deal of pride that the people of Hawaii note that the first non-Caucasian called to serve in the highest councils of world-wide leadership in the LDS Church was Adney Y. Komatsu, a Japanese-American born and raised in Honolulu. The Islands are also the home of Glenn Y. M. Lung, the first Chinese-American bishop, stake president and regional representative. There are hundreds of other local leaders.

As one means of calling attention to the major role that the LDS Church has played in the religious, educational and cultural development of Polynesia, the Hawaii Public Communications Council of The Church of Jesus Christ of Latter-day Saints has published this book featuring a brief history of the Church in Hawaii plus excerpts from the **Book of Mormon** as it was first printed in the Hawaiian language more than 100 years ago. In this day when a new renaissance of interest is arising in the roots of this great state we wish to pay tribute to the proud people who were here when Captain Cook arrived in 1778. Although the Hawaiian language is described by some as dying, we feel it important that a remnant of their writing be preserved in the language which was first used in Hawaii to communicate the teachings of Jesus Christ, the Savior of all men.

Another purpose of this publication is to pay tribute to the early pioneers of the Christian faith in Hawaii of Hawaiian, Asian, European and American heritage. Some of the names are well known: George Q. Cannon, one of the first missionaries to Hawaii; Jonatana Napela, the Hawaiian alii and judge who helped translate the **Book of**

Mormon into the Hawaiian language; Joseph F. Smith, who envisioned the temple at Laie; and the Woolleys who helped to build it.

Along with the Bible, the **Book of Mormon** is a witness of the divinity of Jesus Christ and of the importance and relevance of his teachings in the lives of mankind. In addition, the **Book of Mormon** proclaims that people of the isles of the sea are closely related to their brethren on the North and South American continent as well as other peoples throughout the world. In short, the prophets of the past as well as those of today proclaim that we are all brothers and sisters of a concerned and kind Savior whose primary objective is the immortality and eternal life of man.

ALF PRATTE, Coordinator
Hawaii Public Communications Council

THE CHURCH OF JESUS CHRIST OF LATTER-DAY SAINTS

IN THE HAWAIIAN ISLANDS

Heroic Polynesian navigators led the first settlers to the Hawaiian Islands in the dim centuries before recorded history. They brought with them a highly developed religion and a social system based on inherited rank supported by carefully recited genealogies. A culture developed which was appropriate to and made full use of the island environment. The impact of the discovery, by Captain James Cook, of the islands two hundred years ago was devastating to the carefully balanced island culture. Overnight the ways of the islanders became obsolete and foreign diseases would decimate the population. In the first decade of the Nineteenth Century the island chain was conquered by its first king, Kamehameha I. In quick succession the Hawaiians gave up their old religion, welcomed American Protestant missionaries, received French Catholics and adopted their first constitution.

In 1846 the ship, **Brooklyn**, arrived from New York bound for California. The passengers were Latter-day Saints under the leadership of Samuel Brannan. The protestant newspaper, **The Friend**, gave the first public notice of Mormons in Hawaii and wished the "Mormonites" well in their search for a new home. Four years later, in December of 1850, the **Imaum of Muscat** docked in Honolulu carrying ten young Latter-day Saint missionaries. Elder Hiram Clark was president and, after decicating the islands for the preaching of the Gospel, assigned the elders to labor on the major islands. By the end of the second month, five of the missionaries, including President Clark, had become discouraged and left the islands. The remaining elders preached among the foreign residents, or "whites," and, as they obtained the language, among the Hawaiians. They were successful in both endeavors.

From the beginning, the hospitality and kindness of the Hawaiians was an important factor in the success of the mission. Elders George Q. Cannon and James Keeler were befriended by Nalimanui in Lahaina and welcomed into the home of Jonathon Napela in Wailuku, Maui. Elder Henry W. Bigler stayed with Judge I. W. E. Maikai of Honolulu, and Elder James Farrer was received by J. W. H. Kauwahi, a konohiki (Chiefly land manager). of Koolauloa, Oahu.

Nalimanui
Gave Shelter to First Missionaries — **Lahaina, Maui**

Elder George Q. Cannon

Elders Cannon and Farrer were blessed with the language and were able early to work effectively among the Hawaiians. George Q. Cannon set out from Lahaina on March 1, 1851, feeling impressed that he was setting out to meet friends who were awaiting him. As he arrived in Wailuku, he was invited to stay, and preach, in the home of Jonathon H. Napela, a magistrate of that district. Napela and his wife, the former Kitty Richardson, were both of chiefly rank and risked losing status and perhaps career in thus welcoming the elders. Napela was threatened by some of the local people, so Elder Cannon decided to move to another location. Napela provided the location with an introduction to his property manager in Kula, Maui, a man named Pake. Kaleohano, a relative of Napela, accompanied Elder Cannon to Kula. Within a few days a thatched house

Pulehu Chapel, Maui; Site of First Baptism in Hawaii

had been put up for the preaching services and on Sunday, May 21, 1851, George Q. Cannon preached his first sermon in that building and his first in the Hawaiian language. Shortly afterward Pake, Kaleohano, and Maiola, a deacon in the local church in Kula, were baptized.

By the time Elder Farrer took his second trip to windward Oahu in July of 1851, his friend, Mr. Kauwahi, had moved to Laie. Kauwahi was baptized in August along with a number of others at Hakipuu, Kaaawa, and Kahana. Kaleohano and Kauwahi took up missionary labors almost immediately, accompanying the Utah elders among the people. In a short time the number of converts was such that branches were organized. Elders Keeler and Cannon organized the first branch in Kula, at Kealakou, Maui, on August 6, 1851. Within weeks after this four more were established at Keanae, Waianu, Wailua, and Honomanu on windward East Maui. Hakipuu, on windward Oahu, was organized in October and by the end of the year there were eight branches of the Church in Hawaii, including an interesting one at Makawao, Maui, composed entirely of "whites."

Jonathon Napela and his family were baptized on January 5, 1852 when Elders Cannon and Francis A. Hammond returned from their labors on East Maui. Also baptized at that time were Napela's brother, Kanahunahupu of Waihee and William K. Uaua of Lahaina. Uaua was a prominent resident of West Maui and would later be elected to the legislature of the Kingdom. When a conference was held at Iao, Maui, in April of 1852, Church membership totalled over 700. The principle of the fast and the law of tithing were introduced at this conference and the members were urged to give up smoking. The minutes of this conference also reveal that Elder Cannon, with the support and help of Napela, had begun the translation of the **Book of Mormon** to Hawaiian. This important work would be accomplished in fifteen short months of intermittent labor followed by a careful review by Elders Farrer and Kauwahi on Kauai. Difficulties in printing held up the distribution of

Cannon & Napela Translating the Book of Mormon

the book until April of 1856. Even so, this is regarded by Hawaiian historians as "the miracle" of the founding of Mormonism in Hawaii.

The spirit of the gathering was soon felt in Hawaii with the elders giving attention to searching out an appropriate place as early as 1853. After considering Waimea, Hawaii, and the uplands of Lanai, the process was stopped by a suggestion from America that the newly established colony at San Bernardino, California, be designated as the gathering place for Saints from Hawaii and Tahiti. After some effort in that direction, Lanai was finally chosen and in December of 1854 the "City of Joseph" was laid out at Palawai.

The Saints began to gather as pioneers to Lanai, leaving homes, personal effects, and loved ones to make the move. They prospered there. Joseph F. Smith, a young man on his first mission in Hawaii, sounded a warning. The gathering to Lanai was not an unmixed blessing, he pointed out. The more faithful members were answering the call to Lanai leaving the congregations in a weakened condition and hindering the missionary work. Moreover, those worthy Saints who could not gather at the moment, were becoming badly discouraged. On September 7, 1857, the Utah elders received a letter from President Brigham Young instructing them to return to Utah. The elders departed, the last one in December of that year.

This departure left the mission with serious difficulties. Most of the leadership was concentrated on Lanai. None of the local elders had had more than six or seven years of experience in the Church. Further, the Hawaiian people were less than a generation from their pagan past and few, if any, had made the transition from their early task-oriented interaction with the land and sea for livelihood, to the work-a-day, money economy of the new culture. It was hardly to be expected that the growth of the Church would continue apace.

In the years that followed, problems were encountered which might have led to the eventual loss of the Gospel among the Hawaiians. In June of 1861 Walter Murray Gibson arrived in Honolulu. Exhibiting ornate certificates, "Captain" Gibson proclaimed himself Chief President of The Church of Jesus Christ of Latter-day Saints in the Islands of the Sea. He initiated a number of practices which were clearly contrary to Church policy and was accused of selling offices in the priesthood, among other misdeeds. He later admitted accepting the missionary call as a means to a political end. A number of Hawaiian elders, including Kaleohano, Napela and others, wrote to Salt Lake City reporting on conditions in Hawaii and in March of 1864, a delegation arrived from Utah to address the problem. Ezra T. Benson, Lorenzo Snow, W. W. Cluff, Alma Smith and

Pres. Joseph F. Smith

Joseph F. Smith made up the party. On Lanai, April 7, 1854, Walter Murray Gibson was excommunicated from the Church and Joseph F. Smith was selected to preside over the mission. The Saints on Lanai who wished to remain faithful were urged to leave and return to their original homes.

It was after this conference on Lanai that Elder Lorenzo Snow was drowned in the surf, in a landing accident, off the beach at Lahaina. After an hour's search, his body was recovered and under the hands of the elders and by the power of the priesthood, he was restored to life. Joseph F. Smith, as mission president, set out immediately on a tour of the branches, assisted by Alma Smith. No Saints were found in Lahaina. Most all of the other branches were either weakened or inoperative. The membership of the mission, which had exceeded 4,000 a few years earlier, was now reckoned at just over 1,500.

As early as June of 1859, President Brigham Young had seen the need for aid in stabilizing their economic situation of the Hawaiian Saints. The value of the Lanai experience had undoubtedly been reported in this regard. To serve this end, Elders Francis A. Hammond and George Nebeker were assigned to the islands to purchase property for an agricultural mission. After considering several sites and tentatively deciding on Laie, Elder Nebeker returned to Salt Lake City for approval. In the meantime, Mr. T. Dougherty, the owner of the Laie Ranch, decided that the transaction must be concluded immediately. Elder Hammond was faced with the responsibility of making a decision for the Church. After an anxious night and prayer, he left the ranch house on the property, walked a little distance, and there reported that Presidents Young and Heber C. Kimball appeared to him in vision and indicated that this was the "chosen spot." The property, 6,000 acres with buildings and livestock, was purchased for $14,000. In July of 1865, thirty-eight agricultural missionaries, including children, arrived to put Laie into full operation. Elder George Nebeker returned to preside.

The revival of the mission and the gathering to Laie went slowly. Many Hawaiians were reluctant. They had sacrificed to gather to Lanai, had suffered the Gibson episode and now were being asked to gather again, this time to Laie. Early Laie was not an easy prospect. Drought one year and flooding the next were the expectation. Winds were so strong, so consistent and salt-laden that trees and flowers could not survive. Laie was a sandy, barren plain. Cotton, corn and rice were tried with varying degrees of success. Napela and George Raymond, a half-white early convert, formed a small company and planted some acreage of sugar cane at Hauula, just south of Laie. The success of this venture led to sugar becoming the main crop at the plantation.

Though the agricultural mission was intended to proselyte as well, little attention was given to this until 1868. At the October conference held at Laie, fourteen Hawaiian elders were called to travel and preach among the islands. Napela was placed in charge of this effort. Within the year these missionaries had baptized more than a thousand converts. The policy regarding the use of local elders as missionaries was to change from time to time under different mission presidents but invariably, whenever and wherever these elders were sent, the work prospered.

During the reigns of Kings Kamehameha IV and Kamehameha V, the number of Hawaiians continued to decline. Disease, out-migration, and the race's failure to reproduce itself brought the level so low that in the 1860's it became necessary to consider importing population. The Hawaiians were not necessarily a poor labor force, they were simply insufficient in number. The bringing in of a labor force began in 1865 with the Chinese, followed in 1868 by the first Japanese. Later would come Gilbertese, Portuguese, Koreans, Puerto Ricans, Filipinos and some European peoples, all candidates for the preaching of the gospel.

The King of Hawaii in 1874 was the young and personable Kalakaua whose queen was Kapiolani. On April 22, 1874, the king and queen called, almost by surprise, at Laie on a round-the-island tour. His majesty was entertained by the singing of the children of the plantation school and spoke at some length to the assembled Saints. He expressed a lively interest in the number of children and the ratio of children to adults which, he said, was the highest in the kingdom. He was also impressed with the bearing and appearance of the Hawaiians at Laie. The impression was a lasting one, for both the king and queen returned frequently. Queen Kapiolani unexpectedly visited at a conference held at the Honolulu branch in 1877 and the next day, as Elder Henry P. Richards called at the palace to present the Book of Mormon to the king, she remarked on her enjoyment of the services. The queen's interest in the Church was further evidenced later that year as she happened in at a meeting of the Saints at Honokane, Hawaii. Elder Richards was also there on a mission tour. She recognized him and insisted

Laie Chapel with People Leaving Church — early photo

that he and his companion meet her the next day at Pololu. There she asked Elder Richards to assist her in organizing a female Relief Society among her followers. The queen sponsored this organization, patterned after the women's organization of the Church which had been organized at Laie two years earlier, throughout the islands. Later the queen and her organization was responsible for the founding of a maternity hospital which bears her name. A year later, Queen Kapiolani asked for, and received, an acre of land at Laie, saying she intended to live among the Saints; because, she said, "at Laie my people exhibit their former dignity and self-respect."

Kalakaua came again to Laie for the laying of the cornerstones for the new Laie chapel in 1881 and, by his request, attended and spoke at the dedication of the building two years later. In addition to visits of royalty and the mission conferences held there, life at Laie was enlivened by the Laie Brass Band and the active programs of the Hui Opio (M.I.A.). Sugar, however, was the main business of the plantation and by 1878 twelve to fifteen tons had been milled by the crude mule-driven mill and shipped to Utah for sale. Two years later the first artesian well was drilled on the plantation.

Although the mission and the plantation were relatively successful, living at Laie was hard. Joseph F. Smith, now a member of the First Presidency of the Church, came to Laie in February of 1885 on one of his journeys away from Utah to escape the persecution there because of polygamy. The discouragement of the Saints was seen all around. In a special meeting called for the purpose, President Smith spoke. He prophesied in the name of Israel's God that water would spring from the ground in abundance, that flowers and trees would grow and "that the Glory of the Lord would rest upon the land." More wells were drilled, trees were planted, and improvements were made until King Kalakaua could call it the most attractive village in the kingdom.

In 1893, the monarchy was overthrown and replaced by a republic until annexation could be arranged with the

United States. These momentous developments in history did not attract as much attention in Laie as the completion of the new mission house at Lanihuli, or the close of milling operations at the plantation with the contract for milling to be done at nearby Kahuku. Annexation, which occurred in 1898, was not of as much concern to the Hawaiian Mormons as the migration of island saints to the deserts of Utah where the Hawaiian colony of Iosepa was being set up. The primary reason for this movement was to make the blessing of the temple available to the Hawaiians. The experiment was not totally successful and many of the Hawaiian members returned. It was not many years before Hawaii would have its own temple. It had been prophesied.

At a mission conference at Wailuku, Maui, in 1853, Elder John Woodbury had borne his testimony and spoken in tongues. Elder Hammond interpreted. The natives were the seed of Joseph; the Lord was pleased with the work in the islands, and temples would be built on this land. Joseph F. Smith in 1885 had predicted that "the Glory of the Lord would rest upon the land." In 1900 President George Q. Cannon returned to Hawaii for the mission jubilee and predicted that a temple would be built. President Joseph F. Smith, in Hawaii again in 1915, spoke at a meeting at the Laie Chapel, and afterward retired to the rear of the building to be alone. While there, he was impressed to dedicate the spot for the building of a House of the Lord. At the October conference of the Church that same year, President Smith proposed that a temple be built in Hawaii. Work was commenced three months later and completed on April 18, 1918. William M. Waddoups and his wife, Olivia, arrived at Laie to preside over the temple and on November 13, 1919, President E. Wesley Smith, who was mission president, received a two-word wire from President Heber J. Grant — "Dedication Thirtieth."

President Grant and his party arrived on the twenty-first and the Hawaiian Temple was dedicated on November 27, 1919. The services were held in the upper room of the Temple at 2:30 in the afternoon and repeated on subsequent

Photo by Jim Thorup

Hawaii Temple, April 1978

days. A choir of twelve voices sang and President Grant offered the dedicatory prayer. In the prayer Hawaiians were gratified to hear these words, "We thank Thee for raising up Thy servant, Elder Jonathon H. Napela, that devoted Hawaiian who assisted Thy servant, President Cannon, in the translation of the Book of Mormon..." Temple work was begun in Hawaii the following week.

To this point in time, the activity of the Church in Hawaii had been centered on Maui and at Laie. It is appropriate that the names of some of the early converts be given special mention, lest they be entirely forgotten. Jonathon H. Napela is one of these. His life story is interwoven with the history of the mission. Following nearly twenty years of faithful service, his crowning blessing was to be permitted to travel to Utah and to be endowed at the Endowment House in Salt Lake City in 1869. Perhaps his most severe trial came in 1873 when his beloved Kitty was found to have leprosy. As she was reputed to have been one of the most beautiful women in the kingdom, this was an especially cruel occurrence. Napela went with his wife to the leper settlement at Kalaupapa on Molokai. There he served both the government and the Church among the lepers. The Catholic Father Damien who came to the settlement a year or so later characterized Napela as his "yokemate." Napela died of leprosy at Kalaupapa in 1879 and his wife followed two years later. His final mortal assignment was to preside over the branch at Kalaupapa.

William K. Uaua was one of those greeted by George Q. Cannon at Napela's home on the March evening in 1851. After his baptism he served several short missions. In February of 1853 Uaua was returning from one of these missionary journeys and found his house surrounded by mourners. His wife had been pronounced dead three hours earlier and wailing had already begun. Without hesitation, Uaua entered the house, administered to his wife and restored her to life. This was not an isolated incident in the life of this man. He was well known as one mighty in faith. Uaua was elected to the House of Representatives of the

Jonatana Napela

Kingdom and moved to Honolulu where his preaching attracted crowds of over one thousand, The journals of the Utah elders note that his name meant "cloudburst" and that the name was appropriate because of the power of his preaching. Like many other of the early converts, Uaua was faithful through the Lanai experience and returned to Honolulu where he presided over that conference of the mission. He, with Napela and Kaleohano, were among the "friends" that Elder Cannon felt impressed were awaiting him as he set out to go among the natives in 1851.

An early convert to the Church on Oahu was John W. Kahumoku who, by 1853, had been ordained an elder and assigned with Elder Thomas Karran to labor on Hawaii. Expecting to land at Hilo, the ship was turned back due to bad weather. It was in Kohala that they were finally able to come ashore. Both elders were tired and seasick. Nevertheless, they were met by a large crowd and the people "required that Brother Kahumoku speak to them." He preached for more than an hour and before breakfast the next morning they baptized twenty-five persons. Kohala was one of the strongholds of the protestant ministry. In a short time, however, four branches of the Church were organized. There was trouble and false charges made against the Elders. They were arrested for allegedly interfering with the school over which some local people had charge. Elder Kahumoku, having some acquaintance with the law, defended the case in court. The judge ruled against the Mormons but within a month the judge, the school teacher and nineteen of the twenty-five school children were converted and the missionaries took over the operation of the school. On July 27, 1853, Elder Kahumoku died at the age of 26 after having served only a few weeks in the mission field. Elder Karran testified in his journal that Kahumoku had been called to the world of spirits to preach to his people there. "He is the first of his nation to go to the world of spirits with the priesthood on him. He was one of the most righteous young men I have ever been acquainted with."

Having noted, in passing, some of the valiant among the early Hawaiians, attention may be turned again to the progress of the Church in the islands. With the dedication of the temple, changes began to be made in the affairs of the mission. In 1920, the management of the plantation and the presidency of the mission were made separate functions and a little later mission headquarters was moved to Honolulu. In 1931, the plantation closed and the sugar acreage was leased to the Kahuku Plantation.

President Heber J. Grant returned to Hawaii in June of 1935, and, after touring the islands, examining the problems—leadership, distances, racial mixing, and the insular nature of the territory—and assessing the spirit of the Saints, made the decision to create the Oahu Stake of Zion with its headquarters in Honolulu. A tabernacle for the new stake was built and dedicated in August of 1941. Just before World War II work had begun among the Japanese in Hawaii and this led to the formation fo the Central Pacific Mission through which the gospel message was to be taken to this numerous race. The converts from this mission would later provide bishops, mission and stake presidents and general officers of the Church.

The peoples of Hawaii began to provide missionaries to other parts of the world in the 1860's when Elder Kimo Pelio and three others were sent to the Navigator Islands (Samoa). Elder Pelio died on his mission there but when Elder Joseph H. Dean was called from his second mission in Hawaii to preside over the new mission in that land, there were already converts there. It was from among the members of the Central Pacific Mission that the first missionaries were called when, in 1948, President Edward L. Clissold reopened the Japanese Mission. President Hilton Robertson found his most valuable assistance in Honolulu, also, when he resumed the work in Hong Kong in 1949. From the Souther Far East Mission in Hong Kong, elders from Hawaii were sent to begin the work in the Philippines. Perhaps the most recent development in this regard has been the opening of missionary work in Micronesia in 1976 by the Hawaii Mission, under the direction of President William W. Cannon, a grandson of George Q. Cannon. Elders from Hawaii have played a significant role in this effort.

In early 1955 attention was once again drawn to Laie where, on February 12, President David O. McKay broke ground for a new college for the Church. The founding of the Church College of Hawaii was in fulfillment of a vision and prophecy of President McKay. In 1921, as he visited the mission at Laie, he was inspired by the sight of the flag-raising ceremony at the Church elementary school there. His feelings were articulated the next day on Maui when he indicated that a school of higher learning would be built in Hawaii. The college was established and has since been designated as Brigham Young University Hawaii Campus.

Photo by Frank Kara

Aerial Photograph — Laie, November, 1977

(Bottom to Top): Temple, Student Housing, BYU Hawaii Campus, Polynesian Cultural Center

Its alumni occupy positions of leadership in the Church throughout the Pacific Basin.

The Oahu Stake was divided in August of 1955 to create the Honolulu Stake. In the twenty years which have followed, the growth of the Church in the islands has accelerated as the work of the stake missionaries and the full time missionaries of the Hawaii Mission has been coordinated. In 1962 the Pearl Harbor Stake was formed by a second division of the Oahu Stake, and a stake was organized on the island of Hawaii in 1968. The Honolulu Stake was divided in 1971 and the Kaneohe Stake came into being. A division was made in the Pearl Harbor Stake in 1972 out of which ultimately came the Honolulu West and Waipahu Stakes. Progress on Hawaii justified dividing the Hilo Stake in 1974 from which came the Kona Stake. Maui, Molokai, and Lanai were organized as the Kahului Hawaii Stake in 1975. Two additional stakes were brought into being in 1977 as a campus stake was organized at Brigham Young University Hawaii Campus, and Kauai became a Stake, thus putting all of the Hawaiian Islands under stakes.

The progress of the Church in Hawaii has not been limited to schools and ecclesiastical units. Elder Matthew Cowley addressed a conference meeting at Pulehu, Maui, on July 24, 1947, and referred to a time when people from all of Polynesia would gather in Hawaii near the Temple, each living in a village of its own making. Edward L. Clissold, conferring with a group of college faculty and others in 1959, began to plan a place where the arts and usages of Polynesia might be preserved and demonstrated by students from these cultures. In early stages of the planning, the considerable energies of Wendell B. Mendenhall came into play, and in 1965 the Polynesian Cultural Center was dedicated as an arm of the Church in Hawaii.

In the 1970's the Church began again to place the responsibility for leadership on local Saints. The membership has been blessed and the growth expanded as Hawaiians, Chinese, Japanese, Filipinos, Portuguese,

Samoans, Tongans and other peoples of the islands have taken the lead as local, stake, mission and regional leaders.

Another step in Hawaii's key role in the Pacific was taken in 1976 when the First Presidency announced the creation of the Hawaii-Pacific Islands Area of the Church. Elder John H. Groberg of the First Quorum of Seventy was appointed the first general authority supervisor for the area (which includes all of the stakes and missions in Hawaii, Samoa, Tonga, Fiji and Tahiti) with headquarters in Honolulu. Shortly afterward, additional responsibility was given to Hawaii with the creation of the Presiding Bishoprics Office in Honolulu to care for the needs of the area.

Most accounts of the founding and progress of The Church of Jesus Christ of Latter-day Saints in Hawaii are taken from mission and missionary journals and reflect the concerns and activities of the elders from afar. Without diminishing the stature of these pioneer missionaries and leaders, these pages have deliberately tried to highlight the contributions of the peoples of the islands. The Church has been, for those Hawaiians who would hear the message, their salvation in the spiritual sense. More than this, however, it has been their salvation in a cultural sense as well. Those who have accepted the gospel and been faithful have become the finest examples of their race. The words of Queen Kapiolani come back, "In Laie, my people exhibit their former dignity and self-respect." Truly, the Latter-day Saints have played a significant role in the colorful heritage of Hawaii. Along with the other varied ethnic groups and religions, the LDS people look forward to an equally productive future.

PROVO TEMPLE
THE CHURCH OF JESUS CHRIST
OF LATTER-DAY SAINTS

Excerpts from

The Book of Mormon

in Hawaiian

and

Modern American English

THE

BOOK OF MORMON

An Account Written by

THE HAND OF MORMON UPON PLATES

TAKEN FROM THE PLATES OF NEPHI

Wherefore, it is an abridgment of the record of the people of Nephi, and also of the Lamanites—Written to the Lamanites, who are a remnant of the house of Israel; and also to Jew and Gentile—Written by way of commandment, and also by the spirit of prophecy and of revelation — Written and sealed up, and hid up unto the Lord, that they might not be destroyed—To come forth by the gift and power of God unto the interpretation thereof —Sealed by the hand of Moroni, and hid up unto the Lord, to come forth in due time by way of the Gentile—The interpretation thereof by the gift of God.

An abridgment taken from the Book of Ether also, which is a record of the people of Jared, who were scattered at the time the Lord confounded the language of the people, when they were building a tower to get to heaven —Which is to show unto the remnant of the House of Israel what great things the Lord hath done for their fathers; and that they may know the covenants of the Lord, that they are not cast off forever—And also to the convincing of the Jew and Gentile that JESUS is the CHRIST, the ETERNAL GOD, manifesting himself unto all nations—And now, if there are faults they are the mistakes of men; wherefore, condemn not the things of God, that ye may be found spotless at the judgment-seat of Christ.

TRANSLATED BY JOSEPH SMITH, JUN.

Published by
The Church of Jesus Christ of Latter-day Saints
Salt Lake City, Utah, U.S.A.
1977

ORIGIN OF

THE BOOK OF MORMON

Joseph Smith, through whom, by the gift and power of God, the ancient Scripture, known as THE BOOK OF MORMON, has been brought forth and translated into the English tongue, made personal and circumstantial record of the matter. He affirmed that during the night of September 21, 1823, he sought the Lord in fervent prayer, having previously received a Divine manifestation of transcendent import. His account follows:

"While I was thus in the act of calling upon God, I discovered a light appearing in my room, which continued to increase until the room was lighter than at noonday, when immediately a personage appeared at my bedside, standing in the air, for his feet did not touch the floor.

"He had on a loose robe of most exquisite whiteness. It was a whiteness beyond anything earthly I had ever seen; nor do I believe that any earthly thing could be made to appear so exceedingly white and brilliant. His hands were naked, and his arms also, a little above the wrists; so, also, were his feet naked, as were his legs, a little above the ankles. His head and neck were also bare. I could discover that he had no other clothing on but this robe, as it was open, so that I could see into his bosom.

"Not only was his robe exceedingly white, but his whole person was glorious beyond description, and his countenance truly like lightning. The room was exceedingly light, but not so very bright as immediately around his person. When I first looked upon him, I was afraid; but the fear soon left me.

"He called me by name, and said unto me that he was a messenger sent from the presence of God to me, and that his name was Moroni; that God had a work for me to do; and that my name should be had for good and evil among all nations, kindreds, and tongues, or that it should be both good and evil spoken of among all people.

"He said there was a book deposited, written upon gold plates, giving an account of the former inhabitants of this continent, and the source from whence they sprang. He also said that the fulness of the everlasting Gospel was contained in it, as delivered by the Savior to the ancient inhabitants;

"Also, that there were two stones in silver bows—and these stones, fastened to a breastplate, constituted what is called the Urim and Thummim—deposited with the plates; and the possession and use of these stones were what constituted *Seers* in ancient or former times; and that God had prepared them for the purpose of translating the book.

* * * * * * * *

"Again, he told me, that when I got those plates of which he had spoken—for the time that they should be obtained was not yet fulfilled—I should not show them to any person; neither the breastplate with the Urim and Thummim; only to those to whom I should be commanded to show them; if I did I should be destroyed. While he was conversing with me about the plates, the vision was opened to my mind that I could see the place where

THE TESTIMONY OF THREE WITNESSES

Be It Known unto all nations, kindreds, tongues, and people, unto whom this work shall come: That we, through the grace of God the Father, and our Lord Jesus Christ, have seen the plates which contain this record, which is a record of the people of Nephi, and also of the Lamanites, their brethren, and also of the people of Jared, who came from the tower of which hath been spoken. And we also know that they have been translated by the gift and power of God, for his voice hath declared it unto us; wherefore we know of a surety that the work is true. And we also testify that we have seen the engravings which are upon the plates; and they have been shown unto us by the power of God, and not of man. And we declare with words of soberness, that an angel of God came down from heaven, and he brought and laid before our eyes, that we beheld and saw the plates, and the engravings thereon; and we know that it is by the grace of God the Father, and our Lord Jesus Christ, that we beheld and bear record that these things are true. And it is marvelous in our eyes. Nevertheless, the voice of the Lord commanded us that we should bear record of it; wherefore, to be obedient unto the commandments of God, we bear testimony of these things. And we know that if we are faithful in Christ, we shall rid our garments of the blood of all men, and be found spotless before the judgment-seat of Christ, and shall dwell with him eternally in the heavens. And the honor be to the Father, and to the Son, and to the Holy Ghost, which is one God. Amen.

Oliver Cowdery
David Whitmer
Martin Harris

AND ALSO

THE TESTIMONY OF EIGHT WITNESSES

Be It Known unto all nations, kindreds, tongues, and people, unto whom this work shall come: That Joseph Smith, Jun., the translator of this work, has shown unto us the plates of which hath been spoken, which have the appearance of gold; and as many of the leaves as the said Smith has translated we did handle with our hands; and we also saw the engravings thereon, all of which has the appearance of ancient work, and of curious workmanship. And this we bear record with words of soberness, that the said Smith has shown unto us, for we have seen and hefted, and know of a surety that the said Smith has got the plates of which we have spoken. And we give our names unto the world, to witness unto the world that which we have seen. And we lie not, God bearing witness of it.

Christian Whitmer
Jacob Whitmer
Peter Whitmer, Jun.
John Whitmer
Hiram Page
Joseph Smith, Sen.
Hyrum Smith
Samuel H. Smith

MOKUNA 13.

1. Eia kekahi, olelo mai la ka anela ia'u, i ka i ana, E nana aku! A nana aku la au a ike aku la i na lahuikanaka a me na aupuni he nui wale.

2. A i mai la ka anela ia'u, Ke ike nei oe i ke aha? I aku la au, Ke ike nei au i na lahuikanaka a me na aupuni he nui loa.

3. A i mai la oia ia'u, O lakou nei, oia na lahuikanaka a me na aupuni o ka poe Genetile.

4. E a kekahi, ike aku la au iwaena o na lahuikanaka o ka poe Genetile i ke kahua o kekahi [a]ekalesia nui.

5. A i mai la ka anela ia'u, E nana aku i ke kahua o kahi ekalesia i ino loa ia mamua o na ekalesia e ae a pau, o ka mea ia e [b]pepehi ana i ka poe hoano o ke Akua, he oiaio, a e hoeha ana ia lakou, a e nakii ana ia lakou ilalo, e hooauamo ana ia lakou me kekahi auamo hao, a e lawe ana ia lakou ilalo ma ka noho pio ana.

6. Eia kekahi, ike aku la au i ua ekalesia nui a ino loa la; a ike aku la au o ke [c]diabolo oia ke kahua ona.

7. A ike aku la no hoi au i ke [d]gula, a me ke kala, a me ke kilika, a me ka lole ulaula, a me ka lilina i miloia a nani, a me ka lole maikai o kela ano keia ano, a ike aku la au i na wahine hookamakama he nui wale.

8. A olelo mai la ka anela ia'u, i ka i ana, E nana aku i ke gula, a me ke kala, a me ke kilika, a me ka lole ulaula, a me ka lilina i miloia a nani, a me ka lole maikai, a me na wahine hookamakama, oia ka makemake o ua ekalesia nui a ino loa nei;

9. No ka olelo hoomaikai a ko ke ao nei, i luku ai lakou i ka poe hoano o ke Akua, a lawe ia lakou ilalo ma ka noho pio ana.

10. Eia kekahi, nana aku la au a ike aku la i na [e]kai he nui wale; a hookowa ae la lakou i ka poe Genetile mai ka hua aku a ko'u mau hoahanau.

11. Eia kekahi, i mai la ka anela ia'u, E nana'ku aia no ka inaina o ke Akua maluna o na hua a kou mau hoahanau!

12. A nana aku la au a ike aku la i kekahi [f]kanaka mawaena o ka poe Genetile, ka poe i hookowaia'i mai na hua aku a ko'u

CHAPTER 13.

The nations of the Gentiles—A great and abominable church—America's history foreshadowed—The Bible and the Book of Mormon.

1. And it came to pass that
the angel spake unto me, saying:
Look! And I looked and beheld
many nations and kingdoms.
2. And the angel said unto me:
What beholdest thou? And I
said: I behold many nations
and kingdoms.
3. And he said unto me: These
are the nations and kingdoms of
the Gentiles.
4. And it came to pass that I
saw among the nations of the
Gentiles the foundation of a
[a]great church.
5. And the angel said unto
me: Behold the foundation of a
church which is most abominable
above all other churches, which
[b]slayeth the saints of God, yea,
and tortureth them and bindeth
them down, and yoketh them
with a yoke of iron, and bringeth
them down into captivity.
6. And it came to pass that I
beheld this great and abominable church; and I [c]saw the devil
that he was the foundation of it.
7. And I also [d]saw gold, and
silver, and silks, and scarlets,
and fine-twined linen, and all
manner of precious clothing; and
I saw many harlots.
8. And the angel spake unto
me, saying: Behold the gold, and
the silver, and the silks, and the
scarlets, and the fine-twined
linen, and the precious clothing,
and the harlots, are the desires
of this great and abominable
church.
9. And also for the praise of
the world do they destroy the
saints of God, and bring them
down into captivity.
10. And it came to pass that
I looked and beheld many waters;
and they divided the Gentiles
from the seed of my brethren.
11. And it came to pass that
the angel said unto me: Behold
the wrath of God is upon the
seed of thy brethren.
12. And I looked and beheld a
man among the Gentiles, who
was separated from the seed of
my brethren by the many waters;
and I beheld the Spirit of God,
that it came down and wrought
upon the man; and he went forth
upon the many waters, even
unto the seed of my brethren,
who were in the promised land.

mau hoahanau e na kai he nui loa; a ike aku la au i ka Uhane o
ke Akua, ua iho mai la ilalo a hooikaika iho la maluna o ke kanaka; a holo aku la ia maluna o na kai nui, a hiki aku i na hua a
ko'u mau hoahanau, ka poe e noho ana iloko o ka aina i olelo
mua ia'i.
13. Eia kekahi, ike aku la au i ka Uhane o ke Akua, e hooikaika ana ia maluna o na [g] mea e ae o ka poe Genetile; a holo
aku la lakou mailoko ae o ka noho pio ana, maluna o na kai nui.
14. Eia kekahi, ike aku la au i na kanaka he nui loa o ka
poe Genetile maluna o ka aina i olelo mua ia'i; a ike aku la au i
ka inaina o ke Akua, ua kau ia maluna o na [h] hua a ko'u mau
hoahanau; a ua hoopuehuia lakou imua o ka poe Genetile, a ua
hahauia.
15. A ike aku la au i ka Uhane o ka Haku, maluna ia o ka
poe Genetile; a ua hoopomaikaiia lakou, a loaa iho la ia lakou ka
aina i hooilina no lakou; a ike aku la au ua keokeo lakou, a nani
loa a maikai, e like me [i] ko'u poe kanaka, mamua o ko lakou pepehiia ana.
16. Eia kekahi, ike aku la owau, o Nepai, i ka poe Genetile,
ka poe i hele aku mailoko ae o ka noho pio ana, ua hoohaahaa no
lakou ia lakou iho imua o ka Haku; a o ka mana o ka Haku oia
pu me lakou;
17. A ike aku la au ua houluuluia ko lakou poe [j] makua Genetile maluna o ke kai, a maluna o ka aina no hoi, e kaua ku e ia
lakou;
18. A ike aku la au o ka mana o ke Akua oia pu me lakou; a
o ka inaina o ke Akua maluna no hoi ia o ka poe a pau i houluuluia'ku e kaua ia lakou.
19. A ike aku la wau, o Nepai, ua [k] hoopakeleia aku la ka poe
Genetile, ka poe i hele aku mailoko ae o ka noho pio ana, e ka
mana o ke Akua, mailoko aku o na lima o na aupuni e ae a pau.
20. Eia kekahi, ike aku la au, o Nepai, ua hoopomaikaiia lakou ma ka aina; a ike aku la au i kekahi [l] buke, a ua halihaliia'ku
ia iwaena o lakou.
21. A i mai la ka anela ia'u, Ke ike nei anei oe i ke ano o ka
buke?
22. A i aku la au ia ia, Aole au i ike.
23. A i mai la oia, Aia hoi, e puka ana no ia mailoko ae o ka
waha o kekahi Iudaio. A ike aku la wau, o Nepai, ia buke; a i
mai la oia ia'u, O ka buke au e ike nei, he mooolelo ia o ka poe
Iudaio, a iloko ona i kakauia ai na berita a ka Haku, ana i hana'i i
ko ka hale o Iseraela; a iloko ona no hoi i kakauia ai na wanana
he nui wale a ka poe kaula hemolele; a he mooolelo ia e like me
na mea i kahakahaia maluna iho o na [m] papa keleawe, aka, aole
nae he nui e like me ko na papa; ua kakauia nae iloko ona na

1 NEPHI, 13

13. And it came to pass that I beheld the Spirit of God, that it wrought upon other Gentiles; and they went forth out of captivity, upon the many waters.

14. And it came to pass that I beheld many multitudes of the Gentiles upon the land of promise; and I beheld the wrath of God, that it was upon the seed of my brethren; and they were scattered before the Gentiles and were smitten.

15. And I beheld the Spirit of the Lord, that it was upon the Gentiles, and they did prosper and obtain the land for their inheritance; and I beheld that they were white, and exceeding fair and beautiful, like unto my [i]people before they were slain.

16. And it came to pass that I, Nephi, beheld that the Gentiles who had gone forth out of captivity did humble themselves before the Lord; and the power of the Lord was with them.

17. And I beheld that their mother Gentiles were gathered together upon the waters, and upon the land also, to battle against them.

18. And I beheld that the power of God was with them, and also that the wrath of God was upon all those that were gathered together against them to battle.

19. And I, Nephi, beheld that the [k]Gentiles that had gone out of captivity were delivered by the power of God out of the hands of all other nations.

20. And it came to pass that I, Nephi, beheld that they did prosper in the land; and I beheld a [l]book, and it was carried forth among them.

21. And the angel said unto me: Knowest thou the meaning of the book?

22. And I said unto him: I know not.

23. And he said: Behold it proceedeth out of the mouth of a Jew. And I, Nephi, beheld it; and he said unto me: The book that thou beholdest is a record of the Jews, which contains the covenants of the Lord, which he hath made unto the house of Israel; and it also containeth many of the prophecies of the holy prophets; and it is a record like unto the engravings which are upon the [m]plates of brass, save there are not so many; nevertheless, they contain the covenants of the Lord, which he hath made unto the house of Israel; wherefore, they are of great worth unto the Gentiles.

berita a ka Haku, ana i hana aku ai i ko ka hale o Iseraela; nolaila, ua nui ka maikai o ia mau mea i ka poe Genetile.

24. A i mai la ka anela o ka Haku ia'u, Ua ike aku la oe ua puka mai la ka buke mai ka waha mai o kekahi Iudaio; a ia ia i puka mai ai mai ka waha mai o kekahi Iudaio, ua kakauia iloko ona ka euanelio o ka Haku me ka maopopo, ka mea a na aposetolo he umikumamalua i hoike aku ai; a hoike aku la lakou e like me ka oiaio iloko o ke Keikihipa a ke Akua;

25. Nolaila, puka aku la keia mau mea me ka pololei loa mai ka poe Iudaio aku i ka poe Genetile, e like me ka oiaio iloko o ke Akua;

26. A mahope iho o ka puka ana'ku o ia mau mea ma o ka lima la o ka poe aposetolo he umikumamalua a ke Keikihipa, mai ka poe Iudaio aku i ka poe Genetile, ke ike nei oe i ke kahua o kekahi ekalesia nui a ino loa, i hoopailua loa ia mamua o na ekalesia e ae a pau; no ka mea, aia hoi, ua [n] lawe aku la lakou mai ka euanelio aku o ke Keikihipa, i na mea he nui i moakaka a maikai loa; a me na berita no hoi he nui a ka Haku, ka lakou i lawe aku ai;

27. A ua hana iho la lakou i keia mau mea a pau, e hiki ia lakou ke hookahuli ae i na aoao pololei o ka Haku; a e hiki ia lakou ke hoomakapo a ke hoopaakiki i na naau o na keiki a kanaka;

28. Nolaila, ke ike nei oe a mahope iho o ka hiki ana'ku o ka buke mawaena o na lima o ka ekalesia nui a ino loa, he nui wale na mea moakaka a maikai loa i laweia'ku mai ka buke aku, oia ka buke o ke Keikihipa a ke Akua;

29. A pau keia mau mea moakaka a maikai loa i ka laweia'ku, puka aku la ia i na lahuikanaka a pau o ka poe Genetile; a mahope iho o kona puka ana'ku i na aupuni a pau o ka poe Genetile, he oiaio, i kela aoao o na kai nui au i ike ai me ka poe Genetile i holo aku ai mai ka noho pio ana; ke ike nei oe no ka nui o na mea moakaka a maikai i laweia'ku mailoko aku o ka buke, na mea akaka i ka hoomaopopo ana i na keiki a kanaka, e like me ka moakaka iloko o ke Keikihipa a ke Akua; no keia mau mea i laweia'ku ai mailoko aku o ka euanelio o ke Keikihipa, he nui loa ka poe i hina, he oiaio, a no ia mea, ua nui loa ko Satana mana maluna iho o lakou;

30. Aka hoi, ke ike nei oe o ka [o] poe Genetile i hele ae mai ka noho pio ana, a i hookiekieia iluna e ka mana o ke Akua, maluna iho o na lahuikanaka e ae a pau e noho ana ma ka aina i maikai mamua o na aina e ae a pau, oia ka aina a ka Haku ke Akua i berita ai me kou makuakane, e loaa auanei i kona poe hua i aina hooilina no lakou, aole no lakou la e luku loa i ke koena o [p] kau poe hua i huiia mawaena o kou mau hoahanau;

24. And the angel of the Lord said unto me: Thou hast beheld that the book proceeded forth from the mouth of a Jew; and when it proceeded forth from the mouth of a Jew it contained the plainness of the gospel of the Lord, of whom the twelve apostles bear record; and they bear record according to the truth which is in the Lamb of God.

25. Wherefore, these things go forth from the Jews in purity unto the Gentiles, according to the truth which is in God.

26. And after they go forth by the hand of the twelve apostles of the Lamb, from the Jews unto the Gentiles, thou seest the foundation of a great and abominable church, which is most abominable above all other churches; for behold, they have [n]taken away from the gospel of the Lamb many parts which are plain and most precious; and also many covenants of the Lord have they taken away.

27. And all this have they done that they might pervert the right ways of the Lord, that they might blind the eyes and harden the hearts of the children of men.

28. Wherefore, thou seest that after the book hath gone forth through the hands of the great and abominable church, that there are many plain and precious things taken away from the book, which is the book of the Lamb of God.

29. And after these plain and precious things were taken away it goeth forth unto all the nations of the Gentiles; and after it goeth forth unto all the nations of the Gentiles, yea, even across the many waters which thou hast seen with the Gentiles which have gone forth out of captivity, thou seest—because of the many plain and precious things which have been taken out of the book, which were plain unto the understanding of the children of men, according to the plainness which is in the Lamb of God—because of these things which are taken away out of the gospel of the Lamb, an exceeding great many do stumble, yea, insomuch that Satan hath great power over them.

30. Nevertheless, thou beholdest that the [o]Gentiles who have gone forth out of captivity, and have been lifted up by the power of God above all other nations, upon the face of the land which is choice above all other lands, which is the land that the Lord God hath covenanted with thy father that his seed should have for the land of their inheritance; wherefore, thou seest that the Lord God will not suffer that the Gentiles will utterly destroy the [p]mixture of thy seed, which are among thy brethren.

31. Aole no hoi e ae aku oia i ka poe Genetile e anai loa i na [q]hua a kou mau hoahanau;

32. Aole hoi e ae aku ka Haku ke Akua e noho mau loa ka poe Genetile iloko o ua noho weliweli ana la o ka pouli au e ike nei ia lakou iloko, no ka hunaia ana o na mea moakaka a maikai loa o ka euanelio o ke Keikihipa e ua ekalesia ino loa la, ka mea nona ke kukuluia ana au i ike ai.

33. Nolaila, wahi a ke Keikihipa a ke Akua, e aloha auanei au i ka poe Genetile, ma ka hoopai ana i ke koena o ko ka hale o Iseraela iloko o ka hoopai nui.

34. Eia kekahi, olelo mai la ka anela o ka Haku ia'u, i ka i ana, Aia hoi, wahi a ke Keikihipa a ke Akua, mahope iho o ko'u hoopai ana i ke koena o ko ka hale o Iseraela, a o ua koena nei a'u i olelo ai, oia na hua a kou makuakane; no ia mea, mahope iho o ko'u hoopai ana ia lakou i ka hoopai, a [r]hahauia aku lakou e ka lima o ka poe Genetile; a mahope iho o ko ka poe Genetile hina nui loa ana, no na mea akaka lea a maikai o ka euanelio o ke Keikihipa i hunaia e ua ekalesia ino loa la, oia ka makuwahine o na wahine hookamakama, wahi a ke Keikihipa; e aloha aku no au i ka poe Genetile i kela la, a no ia mea e hoopuka aku no au ia lakou ma o ko'u mana iho, he nui o ko'u euanelio i akaka a i maikai, wahi a ke Keikihipa;

35. No ka mea, aia hoi, i mai la ke Keikihipa, e hoike aku auanei au ia'u iho i kau poe hua, a e kakau auanei lakou i na mea he nui a'u e hana aku ai ia lakou, na mea maopopo a maikai; a mahope iho o ka lukuia ana o kau poe hua a me ka emi ana iloko o ka hoomaloka, a o na hua no hoi a kou mau hoahanau; aia hoi, e [s]hunaia auanei keia mau mea, e puka aku ai i ka poe Genetile, a ma ka haawina a me ka mana o ke Keikihipa e puka aku ai;

36. A iloko o ia mau mea e kakauia'i ko'u euanelio, wahi a ke Keikihipa, a me ko'u pohaku a me ko'u ola;

37. A pomaikai lakou ka [t]poe e imi ana e hoopuka i ko'u Ziona ma ua la la, no ka mea, ia lakou no auanei ka haawina a me ka mana o ka Uhane Hemolele; a ina e hoomau lakou a hiki i ka hopena, e hookiekieia'e auanei lakou ma ka la hope, a e hoolaia iloko o ke aupuni mau loa o ke Keikihipa; a o ka mea nana e hoolaha auanei i ka malu, he oiaio, i na olelo o ka hauoli nui, nani wale auanei lakou maluna o na mauna.

38. Eia kekahi, ike aku la au i ke koena o ka hua a ko'u mau hoahanau, a i ka [u]buke no hoi o ke Keikihipa a ke Akua, ka mea i puka mai, mai ka waha mai o ka Iudaio, a ua hele mai la ia mai ka poe Genetile mai, i ke koena o na hua a ko'u mau hoahanau;

39. A mahope iho o ka puka ana mai o ka buke ia lakou, ike aku la au i [v]na buke e ae, i puka mai ai ma ka mana o ke Keiki-

31. Neither will he suffer that the Gentiles shall destroy the [q]seed of thy brethren.

32. Neither will the Lord God suffer that the Gentiles shall forever remain in that awful state of blindness, which thou beholdest they are in, because of the plain and most precious parts of the gospel of the Lamb which have been kept back by that abominable church, whose formation thou hast seen.

33. Wherefore saith the Lamb of God: I will be merciful unto the Gentiles, unto the visiting of the remnant of the house of Israel in great judgment.

34. And it came to pass that the angel of the Lord spake unto me, saying: Behold, saith the Lamb of God, after I have visited the remnant of the house of Israel—and this remnant of whom I speak is the seed of thy father—wherefore, after I have visited them in judgment, and smitten [r]them by the hand of the Gentiles, and after the Gentiles do stumble exceedingly, because of the most plain and precious parts of the gospel of the Lamb which have been kept back by that abominable church, which is the mother of harlots, saith the Lamb—I will be merciful unto the Gentiles in that day, insomuch that I will bring forth unto them, in mine own power, much of my gospel, which shall be plain and precious, saith the Lamb.

35. For, behold, saith the Lamb: I will manifest myself unto thy seed, that they shall write many things which I shall minister unto them, which shall be plain and precious; and after thy seed shall be destroyed, and dwindle in unbelief, and also the seed of thy brethren, behold, these things shall be [s]hid up, to come forth unto the Gentiles, by the gift and power of the Lamb.

36. And in them shall be written my gospel, saith the Lamb, and my rock and my salvation.

37. And blessed are [t]they who shall seek to bring forth my Zion at that day, for they shall have the gift and the power of the Holy Ghost; and if they endure unto the end they shall be lifted up at the last day, and shall be saved in the everlasting kingdom of the Lamb; and whoso shall publish peace, yea, tidings of great joy, how beautiful upon the mountains shall they be.

38. And it came to pass that I beheld the remnant of the seed of my brethren, and also the [u]book of the Lamb of God, which had proceeded forth from the mouth of the Jew, that it came forth from the Gentiles unto the remnant of the seed of my brethren.

39. And after it had come forth unto them I beheld other [v]books, which came forth by the power of the Lamb, from the Gentiles unto them, unto the convincing of the Gentiles and the remnant of the seed of my brethren, and also the Jews who were scattered upon all the face of the earth, that the records of the prophets and of the twelve apostles of the Lamb are true.

hipa, mai ka poe Genetile mai ia lakou, i ka hoomaopopoia ana o ka poe Genetile, a me ke koena o na hua a ko'u mau hoahanau, a me ka poe Iudaio no hoi, i hoopuehuia'i maluna o ka ili a pau o ka honua, ua oiaio na mooolelo hoike a na kaula a o na aposetolo he umikumamalua a ke Keikihipa.

40. A olelo mai la ka anela ia'u, i ka i ana, E hooiaio auanei keia mau mooolelo hope au i ike ai mawaena o ka poe Genetile, i ka oiaio o na mea [w] mua, oia hoi ka na aposetolo he umikumamalua a ke Keikihipa, a e hoike aku auanei i na mea maopopo a maikai i laweia'ku mai o ua mau mea aku la; a e hoike aku auanei i na ohana, a me na olelo, a me na lahuikanaka, o ke Keikihipa a ke Akua oia ke Keiki a ka Makua mau loa, a o ka Mea e Ola'i no hoi o ko ke ao nei; a he mea e pono ai no na kanaka a pau e hele mai io na la, i ole, aole e hiki ia lakou ke hoolaia.

41. A he mea e pono ai e hele mai lakou e like me na olelo e hookupaaia'na e ka waha o ke Keikihipa: a e hoikeia'ku auanei na olelo a ke Keikihipa iloko o na mooolelo o kau poe hua, a iloko no hoi o na mooolelo o ka poe aposetolo he umikumamalua a ke Keikihipa; nolaila, e [x] hookupaaia laua a elua i hookahi; no ka mea, aia no hookahi Akua a hookahi Kahuhipa maluna iho o ka honua a pau;

42. E hiki mai ana ka manawa e hoike aku ai oia ia ia iho i na lahuikanaka a pau, i ka poe Iudaio, a i ka poe Genetile no hoi; a mahope iho o kona hoike ana'ku ia ia iho i ka poe Iudaio, a i ka poe Genetile no hoi, alaila, e hoike aku oia ia ia iho i ka poe Genetile, a i ka poe Iudaio no hoi, a e lilo ka poe hope i mua, a o ka poe mua i hope.

---

40. And the angel spake unto
me, saying: These last records,
which thou hast seen among the
Gentiles, shall establish the truth
of the [w]first, which are of the
twelve apostles of the Lamb, and
shall make known the plain and
precious things which have been
taken away from them; and shall
make known to all kindreds,
tongues, and people, that the
Lamb of God is the Son of the
Eternal Father, and the Savior
of the world; and that all men
must come unto him, or they
cannot be saved.
41. And they must come according to the words which shall
be established by the mouth of
the Lamb; and the words of the
Lamb shall be made known in
the records of thy seed, as well
as in the records of the twelve
apostles of the Lamb; wherefore
they [x]both shall be established in
one; for there is one God and one
Shepherd over all the earth.
42. And the time cometh that
he shall manifest himself unto
all nations, both unto the Jews
and also unto the Gentiles; and
after he has manifested himself
unto the Jews and also unto the
Gentiles, then he shall manifest
himself unto the Gentiles and
also unto the Jews, and the last
shall be first, and the first shall
be last.

15. Aka hoi, i ka wa e hiki mai ai ia la, wahi a ke kaula, i
[m] hoohaliu hou ole ai lakou i ko lakou naau e ku e i ka Mea Hemolele o ka Iseraela, alaila, e hoomanao oia i na berita, ana i hana mai ai i ko lakou poe kupuna;
16. He oiaio, alaila, e hoomanao oia i na mokupuni o ke kai; a e houluulu no au i na lahuikanaka a pau o ko ka hale o Iseraela, mai na kihi eha o ka honua, wahi a ka Haku, e like me na olelo a ke kaula [n] Zenosa;
17. He oiaio, a e ike ko ke ao nei a pau i ka hoola ana o ka Haku, wahi a ke kaula; a e hoopomaikaiia kela lahui keia lahui, kela ohana keia ohana, kela olelo keia olelo, a me na kanaka a pau.

4. Aia hoi, ua nalowale iho la he nui loa i keia manawa, i ike ole ia e ka poe e noho ana ma Ierusalema. Oiaio, ua alakaiia'ku la ka nui o na ohana a pau; a ua hoopuehuia ma o, a ma o, maluna o na [b] mokupuni o ke kai; a o kahi a lakou i noho ai, aole kekahi o kakou i ike, eia wale no, ua ike kakou ua alakaiia aku lakou.

5. A mahope mai o ke alakaiia ana'ku o lakou, ua wananaia mai la keia mau mea no lakou, a no ka poe a pau e hoopuehuia a e hoohokaia ma neia hope aku, no ka Mea Hemolele o ka Iseraela; no ka mea, e hoopaakiki no lakou i ko lakou mau naau e ku e ia ia; no ia mea, e hoopuehuia'e lakou iwaena o na lahuikanaka a pau, a e inainaia e na kanaka a pau.

6. Aka hoi, mahope iho o ka hanaiia'na o lakou e ka poe [c] Genetile, a i hapai ka Haku i kona lima maluna iho o ka poe Genetile, a i kukulu ia lakou iluna i hae, a i hiiia ka lakou poe keikikane ma ko lakou la mau lima, a i halihaliia ka lakou poe kaikamahine maluna o ko lakou la mau poohiwi, aia hoi, o keia mau mea i oleloia, no ke kino ia; no ka mea, pela io no ka berita a ka Haku i ko kakou poe kupuna kane; a e pili ana ia ia kakou ma na la e hiki mai ana, a me ko kakou poe hoahanau no hoi o ko ka hale o Iseraela.

7. A eia no hoi kekahi ano, e hiki mai ana ka manawa, mahope iho o ka hoopuehuia'na o ko ka hale a pau o Iseraela, e hoala no ka Haku, ke Akua, i kekahi [d] aupuni ikaika, mawaena o ka poe Genetile, he oiaio, maluna iho o ka ili o keia aina, a e [e] hoopuehuia auanei ka kakou poe hua e lakou.

8. A mahope iho o ka hoopuehuia'na o ka kakou poe hua, e hoomaka no ka Haku, ke Akua, [f] e hana i kahi hana kupanaha, iwaena o ka poe Genetile, i kahi hana e pomaikai loa ai auanei ka kakou poe hua; nolaila, ua hoohalikeia ia i ko lakou hanaiia ana e ka poe Genetile, a i ke kaikaiia ana ma ko lakou mau lima, a maluna o ko lakou mau poohiwi.

1 NEPHI, 19

15. Nevertheless, when that day cometh, saith the prophet, that [m]they no more turn aside their hearts against the Holy One of Israel, then will he remember the covenants which he made to their fathers.

16. Yea, then will he remember the isles of the sea; yea, and all the people who are of the house of Israel, will I gather in, saith the Lord, according to the words of the prophet [n]Zenos, from the four quarters of the earth.

17. Yea, and all the earth shall see the salvation of the Lord, saith the prophet; every nation, kindred, tongue and people shall be blessed.

1 NEPHI, 22

4. And behold, there are many who are already lost from the knowledge of those who are at Jerusalem. Yea, the more part of all the tribes have been led away; and they are scattered to and fro upon the [b]isles of the sea; and whither they are none of us knoweth, save that we know that they have been led away.

5. And since they have been led away, these things have been prophesied concerning them, and also concerning all those who shall hereafter be scattered and be confounded, because of the Holy One of Israel; for against him will they harden their hearts; wherefore, they shall be scattered among all nations and shall be hated of all men.

6. Nevertheless, after they shall be nursed by the Gentiles, and the Lord has lifted up his hand upon the [c]Gentiles and set them up for a standard, and their children have been carried in their arms, and their daughters have been carried upon their shoulders, behold these things of which are spoken are temporal; for thus are the covenants of the Lord with our fathers; and it meaneth us in the days to come, and also all our brethren who are of the house of Israel.

7. And it meaneth that the time cometh that after all the house of Israel have been scattered and confounded, that the Lord God will raise up a [d]mighty nation among the Gentiles, yea, even upon the face of this land; and by them shall [e]our seed be scattered.

8. And after our seed is scattered the Lord God will proceed to do a [f]marvelous work among the Gentiles, which shall be of great worth unto our seed; wherefore, it is likened unto their being nourished by the Gentiles and being carried in their arms and upon their shoulders.

MOKUNA 2.

1. Ano, e Iakoba, ke olelo aku nei au ia oe: Ooe no ka'u
[a] hanau mua ma na la o ko'u popilikia iloko o ka waonahele. Aia
hoi ua loohia oe i kou wa kamalii i ka popilikia a me ke kaumaha
nui, no ke kolohe o kou mau hoahanau.
2. Aka hoi, e Iakoba, ka'u hanau mua iloko o ka waonahele,
ke ike nei oe i ka nani o ke Akua; a e hoolaa oia i kou pilikia i
mea nou e pomaikai ai.
3. Nolaila, e hoopomaikaiia kou uhane, a e noho maluhia pu
oe me kou kaikuaana, o Nepai; a e hoolilo ia'ku kou mau la ma
ka hana a kou Akua. Nolaila, ke ike nei au ua hoolapanaiia oe
no ka pono o kou Mea Hoolapanai; no ka mea, ua ike oe e hele
mai ana oia i ka manawa ku pono, e lawe mai i ke ola i kanaka.
4. A ua ike hoi oe i kona nani ma kou wa opiopio; no ia mea,
ua hoopomaikaiia oe e like me ka poe ana e lawelawe mai ai ma
ke kino; no ka mea, oia mau no ka Uhane, inehinei, i keia la, a
mau loa aku. A ua hoomakaukauia ke ala mai ka haule ana mai
o ke kanaka, a ua haawiia mai ke ola mau loa me ka uku ole aku.
5. A ua lawa na kanaka i ke aoia mai, i ike lakou i ka pono
a me ka hewa. A ua haawiia mai ke kanawai i kanaka. A ma
ke kanawai aole i hoaponoia kekahi mea; oia hoi, ma ke kanawai, ua hookiia'ku na kanaka. Oiaio, ma [b] ko ke kino kanawai,
ua hookiia'ku; a ma [c] ko ka uhane kanawai hoi e make ana lakou
mai ka pono aku, a lilo lakou i poe poino a mau loa aku.
6. Nolaila, ke hele mai la ka hoolapanai ana iloko o ka Mesia Hemolele a ma o na la no hoi; no ka mea, ua piha oia i ka
lokomaikai a me ka oiaio.
7. Aia hoi, ke haawi mai la oia ia ia iho i mohai no ka hewa,
e hooko i ka hana a ke kanawai, i ka poe a pau me ka naau palu-
palu a me ka uhane mihi; aole loa e hookoia ka hana a ke kanawai i kekahi mea e ae.
8. Nolaila, he mea nui e hoomaopopo aku i keia mau mea i
ko ke ao nei, i ike lakou aole e hiki i ka io ke noho pu ma ke alo
o ke Akua, ke ole wale no ma ka pono, a me ke aloha, a me ka

CHAPTER 2.

Lehi to his son Jacob—Opposition necessary in all things—The forbidden fruit and the tree of life—Adam fell that men might be—Messiah, the great Mediator, to redeem mankind.

1. And now, Jacob, I speak unto you: Thou art my [a]first-born in the days of my tribulation in the wilderness. And behold, in thy childhood thou hast suffered afflictions and much sorrow, because of the rudeness of thy brethren.

2. Nevertheless, Jacob, my firstborn in the wilderness, thou knowest the greatness of God; and he shall consecrate thine afflictions for thy gain.

3. Wherefore, thy soul shall be blessed, and thou shalt dwell safely with thy brother, Nephi; and thy days shall be spent in the service of thy God. Wherefore, I know that thou art redeemed, because of the righteousness of thy Redeemer; for thou hast beheld that in the fulness of time he cometh to bring salvation unto men.

4. And thou hast beheld in thy youth his glory; wherefore, thou art blessed even as they unto whom he shall minister in the flesh; for the Spirit is the same, yesterday, today, and forever. And the way is prepared from the fall of man, and salvation is free.

5. And men are instructed sufficiently that they know good from evil. And the law is given unto men. And by the law no flesh is justified; or, by the law men are cut off. Yea, by the [b]temporal law they were cut off; and also, by the [c]spiritual law they perish from that which is good, and become miserable forever.

6. Wherefore, redemption cometh in and through the Holy Messiah; for he is full of grace and truth.

7. Behold, he offereth himself a sacrifice for sin, to answer the ends of the law, unto all those who have a broken heart and a contrite spirit; and unto none else can the ends of the law be answered.

8. Wherefore, how great the importance to make these things known unto the inhabitants of the earth, that they may know that there is no flesh that can dwell in the presence of God, save it be through the merits, and mercy, and grace of the Holy Messiah, who layeth down his life according to the flesh, and taketh it again by the power of the Spirit, that he may bring to pass the [d]resurrection of the dead, being the first that should rise.

lokomaikai o ka Mesia Hemolele, nana e waiho aku ilalo i kona ola mamuli o ke kino, a e lawe hou ia mea ma ka mana o ka Uhane, i hiki ia ia ke lawe mai i ke [d]alahou ana o ka poe make, oia no ka mea mua e ala mai ai.

9. Nolaila, oia no ka hua mua i ke Akua, no ka mea, nana e [e]uwao no na keiki a pau a kanaka; a o ka poe a pau e manaoio ia ia e hoolaia lakou.

10. A no ka uwao ia ana no na mea a pau, e hiki aku ana na kanaka a pau i ke Akua la; nolaila, e ku ana lakou ma ke alo ona, e hookolokoloia e ia, e like me ka oiaio a me ka hemolele iloko ona. Nolaila, o ka hope o ke kanawai a ka mea Hemolele i haawi mai ai, i ka hoopai ana i ka uku hoopai i kauia mai, a e kuee ana ua uku hoopai nei i kauia mai, i ka pomaikai i kauia mai, e hooko i ka hope o ke [f]kalahala;

11. No ka mea, ma na mea a pau e [g]kuee ana kekahi aoao i kekahi e pono ai. Ina aole pela, e ka'u hanau mua ma ka waonahele, he mea i hiki ole i ka pono ke hanaia; aole hoi i ka hewa; aole i ka hemolele aole hoi i ka poino; aole i ka maikai aole hoi i ka ino. No ia mea, ina pela e hui pu ia na mea a pau i hookahi; nolaila, ina hookahi kino ia, e waiho ia me he mea make la e pono ai, aole ola aole hoi make, aole palaho aole palaho ole, aole pomaikai aole hoi poino, aole ike aole hoi ike ole.

12. Nolaila, ina pela, ua hanaia mai la ia i mea ole; no ia mea, aole kumu io no ka hanaia'na o ia mea. Nolaila, e hoopau no keia mea i ka naauao o ke Akua, a me kona mau manao paa mau loa, a i ka mana, a i ke aloha, a me ka hoopono ana o ke Akua no hoi.

13. A ina e i aku oukou aole he kanawai, e i no hoi oukou aole he hewa. A ina e olelo oukou aole he hewa, e olelo no hoi oukou aole no he pono. A ina aole he pono, aole hoi he pomaikai. A ina aole he pono, aole hoi he pomaikai, alaila, aole he hoopai aole hoi he poino. A ina aole keia mau mea, aole he Akua. A ina aole he Akua, aole o kakou, aole hoi ka honua; no ka mea, aole i hiki ke hanaia kekahi mea, aole e hana aku, aole hoi e hanaia mai; nolaila, ina ua nalowale iho na mea a pau.

14. Ano, e ka'u mau keiki, ke olelo aku nei au i keia mau mea, no ko oukou pomaikai a hoonaauaoia'na; no ka mea, aia no he Akua, a ua hana mai la oia i na mea a pau, ma ka lani a ma ka honua no hoi, a me na mea a pau oloko; o na mea e hana aku, a me na mea e hanaia mai;

15. A no ka hooko ana i kona manao mau loa i ka hana ana i kanaka, mahope iho o kana hana ana i ko kakou mau kupuna

9. Wherefore, he is the first-fruits unto God, inasmuch as he shall make [e]intercession for all the children of men; and they that believe in him shall be saved.

10. And because of the intercession for all, all men come unto God; wherefore, they stand in the presence of him to be judged of him according to the truth and holiness which is in him. Wherefore, the ends of the law which the Holy One hath given, unto the inflicting of the punishment which is affixed, which punishment that is affixed is in opposition to that of the happiness which is affixed, to answer the ends of the [f]atonement—

11. For it must needs be, that there is an [g]opposition in all things. If not so, my first-born in the wilderness, righteousness could not be brought to pass, neither wickedness, neither holiness nor misery, neither good nor bad. Wherefore, all things must needs be a compound in one; wherefore, if it should be one body it must needs remain as dead, having no life neither death, nor corruption nor incorruption, happiness nor misery, neither sense nor insensibility.

12. Wherefore, it must needs have been created for a thing of naught; wherefore there would have been no purpose in the end of its creation. Wherefore, this thing must needs destroy the wisdom of God and his eternal purposes, and also the power, and the mercy, and the justice of God.

13. And if ye shall say there is no law, ye shall also say there is no sin. If ye shall say there is no sin, ye shall also say there is no righteousness. And if there be no righteousness there be no happiness. And if there be no righteousness nor happiness there be no punishment nor misery. And if these things are not there is no God. And if there is no God we are not, neither the earth; for there could have been no creation of things, neither to act nor to be acted upon; wherefore, all things must have vanished away.

14. And now, my sons, I speak unto you these things for your profit and learning; for there is a God, and he hath created all things, both the heavens and the earth, and all things that in them are, both things to act and things to be acted upon.

15. And to bring about his eternal purposes in the end of man, after he had created our first parents, and the beasts of the field and the fowls of the air, and in fine, all things which are created, it must needs be that there was an [h]opposition; even the forbidden fruit in opposition to the tree of life; the one being sweet and the other bitter.

mua, a me na holoholona o ke kula a me na manu o ka lewa, a
me na mea a pau i hanaia, he mea pono ke kauia mai he mau
mea [h]kuee; oia ka hua i papaia e kuee ana i ka laau o ke ola;
o kekahi he ono ia, a o kekahi he awaawa;
16. Nolaila, haawi mai la ke Akua i kanaka, i hiki ia ia ke
hana e like me kona manao iho. Nolaila, ua hiki ole i ke kanaka
ke hana e like me kona manao iho, ke hoowalewale ole ia oia e
kela, a i ole ia, e keia.
17. A ke manao nei au, o Lehi, e like me na mea a'u i heluhelu ai, ua haule kekahi anela o ke Akua, mai ka lani mai, e like
me [i]ka mea i palapalaia; nolaila, lilo iho la oia i diabolo, no kona imi ana i ka mea hewa imua o ke Akua.
18. A no kona haule ana mai ka lani mai, a lilo ana i mea poino
no ka wa pau ole, imi iho la no hoi oia, i ka poino o na kanaka
a pau. Nolaila, i ae la oia, o kela nahesa kahiko, oia ke diabolo,
oia hoi ka makuakane o na mea wahahee a pau, ia Ewa; nolaila,
i ae la oia, E ai i ka hua i papaia, aole olua e make, aka e like
auanei olua me ke Akua, i ka ike ana i ka pono a me ka hewa.
19. A mahope iho o ko Adamu laua me Ewa ai ana i ka hua i
papaia, ua kipakuia aku la laua iwaho o ka mahinaai o Edena, e
mahi i ka honua.
20. A ua hanau mai la laua i na keiki; he oiaio, i ka ohana o
ko ke ao nei a pau.
21. A ua hooloihiia na la o na keiki a kanaka, e like me ka
makemake o ke Akua, i hiki ia lakou ke mihi oiai lakou ma ke
kino; nolaila, lilo mai la ko lakou noho ana i noho ana e hoaoia'i,
a ua hooloihiia ko lakou manawa, e like me na kauoha a ke Akua
i haawi mai ai i na keiki a kanaka. No ka mea, haawi mai la oia
i kauoha no na kanaka a pau e mihi lakou e pono ai; a hoike mai
la no hoi oia i na keiki a kanaka a pau ua lilo aku la lakou, no
ka hala o na kupuna mua o lakou.
22. Ano, aia hoi, ina aole o Adamu i hana i ka hala, ina aole
oia i haule; aka, ina ua noho oia ma ka mahinaai o Edena; a ina
ua oia mau na mea a pau i hanaia'i, ma ko lakou ano mua, mahope mai o ko lakou hanaia'na; a ina ua waihoia mai la lakou
a mau loa aku, aole hoi hopena.
23. [j]Aole hoi laua e hanau i na keiki; nolaila, ua noho laua i
ka noho hala ole ana, aole hauoli, no ka mea, aole o laua i ike i
ka poino; aole e hana ana i ka pono, no ka mea, aole o laua i ike
i ka hewa.
24. Aka hoi, ua hanaïa mai la na mea a pau ma ka naauao o
ka mea nana i ike i na mea a pau loa.
25. [k]Haule iho la o Adamu, i loaa ai na kanaka; a ke ola nei
na kanaka, i loaa ai ia lakou ka olioli.
26. Ke hele mai la ka Mesia i ka manawa ku pono, e hiki ia

16. Wherefore, the Lord God gave unto man that he should act for himself. Wherefore, man could not act for himself save it should be that he was enticed by the one or the other.

17. And I, Lehi, according to the things which I have read, must needs suppose that an angel of God, according to that [i]which is written, had fallen from heaven; wherefore, he became a devil, having sought that which was evil before God.

18. And because he had fallen from heaven, and had become miserable forever, he sought also the misery of all mankind. Wherefore, he said unto Eve, yea, even that old serpent, who is the devil, who is the father of all lies, wherefore he said: Partake of the forbidden fruit, and ye shall not die, but ye shall be as God, knowing good and evil.

19. And after Adam and Eve had partaken of the forbidden fruit they were driven out of the garden of Eden, to till the earth.

20. And they have brought forth children; yea, even the family of all the earth.

21. And the days of the children of men were prolonged, according to the will of God, that they might repent while in the flesh; wherefore, their state became a state of probation, and their time was lengthened, according to the commandments which the Lord God gave unto the children of men. For he gave commandment that all men must repent; for he showed unto all men that they were lost, because of the transgression of their parents.

22. And now, behold, if Adam had not transgressed he would not have fallen, but he would have remained in the garden of Eden. And all things which were created must have remained in the same state in which they were after they were created; and they must have remained forever, and had no end.

23. And they would have had [j]no children; wherefore they would have remained in a state of innocence, having no joy, for they knew no misery; doing no good, for they knew no sin.

24. But behold, all things have been done in the wisdom of him who knoweth all things.

25. Adam [k]fell that men might be; and men are, that they might have joy.

ia ke hoola i na keiki a kanaka mai ka haule ana mai. A no ko lakou hoolaia'na mai ka haule ana mai, ua lilo lakou i poe 'kuokoa a mau loa aku, e ike ana i ka pono a me ka hewa; e hana no lakou iho, aole e hanaia mai, ma ka hoopai ana o ke kanawai wale no, ma ka la nui mahope, e like me na kauoha a ke Akua i haawi mai ai.

27. Nolaila, mamuli o ke kino ua kuokoa na kanaka; a ua haawiia mai la na mea a pau ia lakou i ku pono i kanaka. A ua noa lakou e koho aku i ka noho pio ole a me ke ola mau loa, ma o ka Mea Uwao nui la o na kanaka a pau; a i ole ia, e koho i ka noho pio a me ka make, e like me ka noho pio ana a me ka mana o ke diabolo; no ka mea, ke imi nei oia i poino pu na kanaka a pau e like me ia iho.

28. Ano, e ka'u mau keiki, ke makemake nei au e nana oukou i ka Mea Uwao nui, a e hoolohe i kana mau kauoha nui; a e malama pono i kana mau olelo, a e koho aku i ke ola mau loa, e like me ka makemake o kona Uhane Hemolele.

29. Aole e koho aku i ka make mau loa, e like me ka makemake o ke kino a me ka hewa koloko, oia na mea e haawi aku ana i ka uhane o ke diabolo i ka mana e hoopio, a e lawe ia oukou ilalo i gehena, i hiki ia ia ke noho alii maluna o oukou iloko o kona aupuni.

30. Ua olelo aku au i keia mau olelo kakaikahi ia oukou a pau, e a'u mau keiki, ma na la hope o kuu hoaoia ana; a ua koho au i ka mea e pono ai, e like me na olelo a ke kaula. A o ko'u manao wale no, o ke ola mau loa no ia o ko oukou mau uhane. Amene.

---

2 NEPHI, 2

26. And the Messiah cometh in the fulness of time, that he may redeem the children of men from the fall. And because that they are redeemed from the fall they have become free forever, knowing good from evil; to act for themselves and not to be acted upon, save it be by the punishment of the law at the great and last day, according to the commandments which God hath given.

27. Wherefore, men are free according to the flesh; and all things are given them which are expedient unto man. And they are free to choose liberty and eternal life, through the great mediation of all men, or to choose captivity and death, according to the captivity and power of the devil; for he seeketh that all men might be miserable like unto himself.

28. And now, my sons, I would that ye should look to the great Mediator, and hearken unto his great commandments; and be faithful unto his words, and choose eternal life, according to the will of his Holy Spirit;

29. And not choose eternal death, according to the will of the flesh and the evil which is therein, which giveth the spirit of the devil power to captivate, to bring you down to hell, that he may reign over you in his own kingdom.

30. I have spoken these few words unto you all, my sons, in the last days of my probation; and I have chosen the good part, according to the words of the prophet. And I have none other object save it be the everlasting welfare of your souls. Amen.

MOKUNA 9.

1. Ano, e o'u mau hoahanau i alohaia, ua heluhelu au i keia
mau mea, i ike ai oukou no na berita a ka Haku, ana i berita mai
ai me ko ka hale a pau o Iseraela;
2. I oleloia mai la e ia i ka poe Iudaio, ma ka waha o kana
poe kaula hemolele, mai kinohou mai, mai kahi hanauna mai i
kahi hanauna, a hiki mai ka manawa e [a] hoihoiia ai lakou i ka ekalesia oiaio a ohana hoi o ke Akua; i ka wa a lakou e houluuluia'i
i ko lakou aina hooilina, a e hookupaaia ma ko lakou mau aina a
pau i hai mua ia'i.
3. Aia hoi, e na hoahanau i alohaia o'u, ke olelo aku nei au
ia oukou i keia mau mea i hauoli ai oukou, a i hapai ai i ko oukou
mau poo no ka wa pau ole, no na mea e pomaikai ai a ka Haku e
haawi mai ai auanei maluna o ka oukou poe hua.
4. No ka mea, ua ike au ua imi nui kekahi poe o oukou, e
ike i na mea e hiki mai ana; nolaila, ke ike nei au ua ike oukou
e mae aku ko kakou io a e make; aka hoi, ma ko kakou [b] mau
kino e ike ai kakou i ke Akua.
5. Oiaio, ke ike nei au ua ike oukou, ma ke kino e hoike aku
ai oia ia ia iho i ka poe e noho ana ma Ierusalema, mai kahi a
kakou i hele mai nei; no ka mea, he mea e pono ai e hiki ia mea
iwaena o lakou; no ka mea, he mea pono no ka Mea nui nana i
hana i na mea a pau, e hookuu aku ia ia iho e lilo malalo o kanaka ma ka io, a e [c] make no na kanaka a pau, i lilo na kanaka a
pau malalo iho ona.
6. No ka mea, e like me ka hooiliia'na o ka make maluna o
na kanaka a pau, pela hoi he mana o ke alahouana e pono ai, e
hooko i ke kumu-manao aloha o ka Mea nui nana i hana i na mea
a pau, a [d] e hiki mai ke alahouana i kanaka e pono ai no ka haule
ana; a ua hiki mai ka haule ana no ka lawehala; a no ka haule
ana o kanaka, ua hookiia'ku la lakou [e] mai ke alo aku o ka Haku;
7. Nolaila, ea, he [f] kalahala mana loa e pono ai; ke ole he
kalahala mana loa, ua hiki ole i keia palaho ke aahu i ka palaho
ole. No ia mea la, o ka [g] hoopai mua ana i hiki maluna iho o kanaka, ua mau loa ia maluna ona, ia ao aku ia ao aku. A ina
pela, ua moe ilalo no keia io e palaho, a e lilo hou i kona lepo makua, aole ala hou mai.
8. E! ka naauao o ke Akua! Kona aloha a lokomaikai!
No ka mea, ina aole e ala hou ka io, e lilo no ko kakou poe uhane
malalo iho o kela [h] anela, ka mea i haule iho mai ke alo iho o ke
Akua mau loa, a lilo iho la i diabolo, e pii hou ole ai;
9. A ina ua lilo ko kakou poe uhane [i] e like pu me ia, a ina

CHAPTER 9.

Jacob's teachings continued—The infinite atonement—The Savior's sufferings foreseen—Where there is no law there is no punishment.

1. And now, my beloved brethren, I have read these things that ye might know concerning the covenants of the Lord that he has covenanted with all the house of Israel—

2. That he has spoken unto the Jews, by the mouth of his holy prophets, even from the beginning down, from generation to generation, until the time comes that they shall be [a]restored to the true church and fold of God; when they shall be gathered home to the lands of their inheritance, and shall be established in all their lands of promise.

3. Behold, my beloved brethren, I speak unto you these things that ye may rejoice, and lift up your heads forever, because of the blessings which the Lord God shall bestow upon your children.

4. For I know that ye have searched much, many of you, to know of things to come; wherefore I know that ye know that our flesh must waste away and die; nevertheless, in our [b]bodies we shall see God.

5. Yea, I know that ye know that in the body he shall show himself unto those at Jerusalem, from whence we came; for it is expedient that it should be among them; for it behooveth the great Creator that he suffereth himself to become subject unto man in the flesh, and [c]die for all men, that all men might become subject unto him.

6. For as death hath passed upon all men, to fulfil the merciful plan of the great Creator, there must needs be a power of resurrection, and the [d]resurrection must needs come unto man by reason of the fall; and the fall came by reason of transgression; and because man became fallen they were cut off [e]from the presence of the Lord.

7. Wherefore, it must needs be an infinite [f]atonement—save it should be an infinite atonement this corruption could not put on incorruption. Wherefore, the [g]first judgment which came upon man must needs have remained to an endless duration. And if so, this flesh must have laid down to rot and to crumble to its mother earth, to rise no more.

8. O the wisdom of God, his mercy and grace! For behold, if the flesh should rise no more our spirits must become subject to that [h]angel who fell from before the presence of the Eternal God, and became the devil, to rise no more.

ua lilo kakou i poe diabolo, he poe anela i ke diabolo, e hooku-
keia iwaho mai ke alo aku o ko kakou Akua, a e noho pu me ka
makua o na wahahee, ma ka poino, e like me ia iho; he oiaio, i
kela mea nana i hoowalewale i ko kakou mau kupuna mua; ka
mea e hoolilo ana ia ia iho, aneane e like me kahi anela o ka malamalama, a e paipai ana i na naau o na keiki a kanaka ma ka
huipumalu ana o ka pepehi kanaka, a i na hana huna o ka pouli
o kela ano keia ano.
10. E! nani ke aloha o ko kakou Akua, nana i hoomakaukau
i ala no ko kakou pakele ana, mai ka puliki ana mai o keia mea
nui weliweli; he oiaio, kela mea nui weliweli, o ka [j]make a me
ka po, a'u i kapa aku ai ka make o ke kino, a ka make hoi o ka
uhane.
11. A no ke ala o ko kakou Akua, ka Mea Hemolele o ka Iseraela, e pakele ai, o keia make, a'u i olelo ai, oia ko ke kino
make, e haawi mai ia i kona poe i make; a o ua make nei oia no
ka lua kupapau.
12. A o keia make a'u i olelo ai, o ko ka uhane make ia, e
haawi mai no auanei ia i kona poe make; a o ua make nei oia no
ka po; nolaila, e haawi mai no ka [k]make me ka po i ko laua poe
i make e pono ai, a e haawi mai ka po i kona poe uhane i pio, a e
haawi mai ka lua kupapau i kona poe kino i pio, a e hoihoi hou
pu ia na kino a me na uhane o kanaka, kekahi i kekahi; a ma o
ka mana la o ke alahouana o ka Mea Hemolele o ka Iseraela
ia mea.
13. E! nani ke kumu-manao o ko kakou Akua! No ka mea,
eia hoi, e haawi mai ka [l]paradaiso o ke Akua i na uhane o ka
poe pono e pono ai, a o ka lua kupapau hoi e haawi mai ia i na
kino o ka poe pono; a [m]e hui pu hou ia ka uhane a me ke kino,
a e lilo na kanaka a pau i palaho ole, a i make ole, a he poe kino-
uhane ola lakou, i loaa ka ike paka e like me kakou nei, ma ke
kino; eia ka like ole, e akaka lea loa auanei ko kakou ike ia
manawa;
14. Nolaila, e loaa ia kakou ka [n]ike lea no ko kakou mau hewa
a pau, a me ko kakou haumia, a me ko kakou kohana; a e loaa
i ka poe pono ka ike lea no ko lakou pomaikai, a me ko lakou pono,
i aahuia me ka hemolele, he oiaio, me ka aahu o ka pono.
15. Eia kekahi, i ka wa i hele aku ai na kanaka a pau mai
keia make mua aku i ke ola, i ko lakou lilo ana i ka make ole, e
ku no auanei lakou imua o ka noho hookolokolo o ka Mea Hemolele o ka Iseraela; alaila e hiki mai ka hooponopono ana, a, alaila e hookolokoloia lakou e like me ka hooponopono hemolele ana
o ke Akua.
16. A oiaio iho la, ma ke ola ana o ka Haku, no ka mea, ua

9. And our spirits must have become [i]like unto him, and we become devils, angels to a devil, to be shut out from the presence of our God, and to remain with the father of lies, in misery, like unto himself; yea, to that being who beguiled our first parents, who transformeth himself nigh unto an angel of light, and stirreth up the children of men unto secret combinations of murder and all manner of secret works of darkness.

10. O how great the goodness of our God, who prepareth a way for our escape from the grasp of this awful monster; yea, that monster, [j]death and hell, which I call the death of the body, and also the death of the spirit.

11. And because of the way of deliverance of our God, the Holy One of Israel, this death, of which I have spoken, which is the temporal, shall deliver up its dead; which death is the grave.

12. And this death of which I have spoken, which is the spiritual death, shall deliver up its dead; which spiritual death is hell; wherefore, [k]death and hell must deliver up their dead, and hell must deliver up its captive spirits, and the grave must deliver up its captive bodies, and the bodies and the spirits of men will be restored one to the other; and it is by the power of the resurrection of the Holy One of Israel.

13. O how great the plan of our God! For on the other hand, the [l]paradise of God must deliver up the spirits of the righteous, and the grave deliver up the body of the righteous; and the spirit and the body is [m]restored to itself again, and all men become incorruptible, and immortal, and they are living souls, having a perfect knowledge like unto us in the flesh, save it be that our knowledge shall be perfect.

14. Wherefore, we shall have a [n]perfect knowledge of all our guilt, and our uncleanness, and our nakedness; and the righteous shall have a perfect knowledge of their enjoyment, and their righteousness, being clothed with purity, yea, even with the robe of righteousness.

15. And it shall come to pass that when all men shall have passed from this first death unto life, insomuch as they have become immortal, they must appear before the judgment-seat of the Holy One of Israel; and then cometh the judgment, and then must they be judged according to the holy judgment of God.

olelo mai ka Haku ke Akua ia mea, a o kana olelo mau loa ia, i hiki ole ke haule wale; a o ka poe i pono, e mau no ko lakou pono, a o ka poe i paumaele, [o] e mau no ko lakou paumaele; nolaila, o ka poe i paumaele, oia no ke diabolo a me kona poe anela; a e hele aku no lakou i ke ahi pio ole, i hoomakaukauia no lakou; a o ko lakou ehaeha me he loko ahi la a me ke kukae pele ia, a o kona lapalapa e pii ana ia, ia ao aku ia ao aku, aohe ona hopena.

17. E! ka nani a me ka pololei o ko kakou Akua! No ka mea, e hooko ana oia i kana mau olelo a pau, a ua hele aku la ia mau mea mailoko mai o kona waha, a e hookoia kona mau kanawai.

18. Aka, aia hoi, o ka poe pono, ka poe hoano o ka Mea Hemolele o ka Iseraela, o ka poe i manaoio i ka Mea Hemolele o ka Iseraela, o ka poe i hoomanawanui i na mea keakea o ko ke ao nei, a i hoowahawaha i ka hoohilahila mai ona; e loaa auanei ia lakou ke aupuni o ke Akua, i hoomakaukauia no lakou [p] mai ka hookumuia'na mai o ke ao nei, a e piha auanei lakou i ka hauoli no ka wa pau ole.

19. E! ka nani o ka lokomaikai o ko kakou Akua, ka Mea Hemolele o ka Iseraela! No ka mea, ke hoopakele mai la oia i kona poe hoano mai [q] kela mea ino weliweli mai o ke diabolo, a me ka make a me ka po no hoi, a me kela loko ahi a me ke kukae pele, oia no ka ehaeha pau ole.

20. E! nani loa ka hemolele o ko kakou Akua! No ka mea, ke ike nei oia i [r] na mea a pau, aohe kekahi mea, i ike ole ia e ia.

21. A e hele mai ana oia i ke ao nei i hiki ia ia ke hoola i na kanaka a pau, ke hoolohe lakou i kona leo; no ka mea, aia hoi, e loaa ana ia ia [s] na eha o na kanaka a pau; he oiaio, na eha o kela mea ola o keia mea ola, o na kane, na wahine, a me na keiki, e pili ana i ka ohana a Adamu.

22. A e loaa keia ia ia, i loaa i na kanaka a pau ke [t] alahouana, e hiki ia lakou a pau ke ku imua ona, ma ka la hookolokolo nui.

23. A ke kauoha mai la oia i na kanaka a pau, [u] e mihi lakou e pono ai, a e bapetizoia ma kona inoa, me ka manaoio ikaika i ka Mea Hemolele o ka Iseraela, i ole ia, e hiki ole ai ia lakou ke hoolaia iloko o ke aupuni o ke Akua.

24. A ina aole lakou e mihi a e manaoio aku i kona inoa, a e bapetizoia ma kona inoa, a e hoomau a hiki i ka hopena, e hoohewaia lakou e pono ai; no ka mea, ua olelo mai la ka Haku ke Akua, ka Mea Hemolele o ka Iseraela, ia mea;

16. And assuredly, as the Lord liveth, for the Lord God hath spoken it, and it is his eternal word, which cannot pass away, that they who are righteous shall be righteous still, and they who are filthy shall be [o]filthy still; wherefore, they who are filthy are the devil and his angels; and they shall go away into everlasting fire; prepared for them; and their torment is as a lake of fire and brimstone, whose flame ascendeth up forever and ever and has no end.

17. O the greatness and the justice of our God! For he executeth all his words, and they have gone forth out of his mouth, and his law must be fulfilled.

18. But, behold, the righteous, the saints of the Holy One of Israel, they who have believed in the Holy One of Israel, they who have endured the crosses of the world, and despised the shame of it, they shall inherit the kingdom of God, which was prepared for them [p]from the foundation of the world, and their joy shall be full forever.

19. O the greatness of the mercy of our God, the Holy One of Israel! For he delivereth his saints from that [q]awful monster the devil, and death, and hell, and that lake of fire and brimstone, which is endless torment.

20. O how great the holiness of our God! For he knoweth all [r]things, and there is not anything save he knows it.

21. And he cometh into the world that he may save all men if they will hearken unto his voice; for behold, he suffereth the pains of all men, yea, the [s]pains of every living creature, both men, women, and children, who belong to the family of Adam.

22. And he suffereth this that the [t]resurrection might pass upon all men, that all might stand before him at the great and judgment day.

23. And he commandeth all men that [u]they must repent, and be baptized in his name, having perfect faith in the Holy One of Israel, or they cannot be saved in the kingdom of God.

24. And if they will not repent and believe in his name, and be baptized in his name, and endure to the end, they must be damned; for the Lord God, the Holy One of Israel, has spoken it.

25. Nolaila, ua haawi mai la oia i kanawai; a ma kahi i haawi ole ia i kanawai, aohe he hoopai ana; a ma kahi o ka hoopai ole ana, aohe he hoohewa ana; a ma kahi o ka hoohewa ole ana, e hoomalu ana na mea aloha o ka Mea Hemolele o ka Iseraela maluna o lakou, no ke [v] kalahala ana; no ka mea, ua hoopakeleia lakou e ka mana ona;

26. No ka mea, e hooluolu ana ke kalahala i ka hookoia ana o kona hoopai maluna o ka poe a pau i haawi ole ia mai ke kanawai ia lakou, a ua hoopakeleia lakou mai kela mea nui weliweli, o ka [w] make a me ka po, a me ke diabolo, a me ka loko ahi a me ke kukae pele, oia ka ehaeha pau ole; a e hoihoi hou ia lakou i kela Akua nana i haawi mai ia lakou i ka hanu, oia ka Mea Hemolele o ka Iseraela.

27. Aka, auwe ka mea i haawiia mai ke kanawai ia ia; he oiaio, ka mea i loaa na kauoha a pau a ke Akua, e like me kakou nei, a e ae maluna o ia mau mea, a e hoomaunauna ana i na la o kona noho hoaoia ana; no ka mea, ua weliweli kona noho ana!

28. E! ka hana maalea o ka mea ino! E! ka haaheo, a me ka nawaliwali, a me ka lapuwale o kanaka! Ia lakou i [x] aoia'i, manao iho la lakou ua naauao, aole lakou e hoolohe i ka olelo ao a ke Akua, no ka mea, waiho wale lakou ia mea e kuhi ana ua ike lakou no lakou iho. Nolaila, ua lapuwale ko lakou ike, aole ia he mea e pono ai lakou. A e make no lakou.

29. Aka, ua maikai ke aoia, ke hoolohe lakou i na olelo ao a ke Akua.

30. Aka, auwe ka poe waiwai, ka poe i waiwai ma na mea o ke ao nei. No ko lakou waiwai, ke hoowahawaha nei lakou i ka poe hune, a hoomaau no lakou i ka poe akahai, a ua kauia ko lakou mau naau maluna o ko lakou waiwai; nolaila, o ko lakou waiwai he Akua ia no lakou. Aia hoi, e make pu auanei ko lakou waiwai me lakou hoi.

31. A, auwe ka poe hookuli, e hoolohe ole mai ana; no ka mea, e make no lakou.

32. Auwe ka poe makapo, e nana ole mai ana; no ka mea, e make no hoi lakou.

33. Auwe ka poe i okipoepoe ole ia ma ka naau; no ka mea, e hoowalania ka ike o ka lakou hana ino ia lakou ma ka la hope.

34. Auwe ka mea wahahee; no ka mea, e hahaoia oia ilalo i gehena.

35. Auwe ka mea pepehi kanaka, nana i pepehi me ka noonoo e; no ka mea, e make ia.

36. Auwe ka poe e [y] moekolohe ana; no ka mea, e hahaoia lakou ilalo i gehena.

37. Oiaio, auwe ka poe i hoomana i na kii; no ka mea, e lealea ana ke diabolo o na diabolo a pau ia lakou.

25. Wherefore, he has given a law; and where there is no law given there is no punishment; and where there is no punishment there is no condemnation; and where there is no condemnation the mercies of the Holy One of Israel have claim upon them, because of the [v]atonement; for they are delivered by the power of him.

26. For the atonement satisfieth the demands of his justice upon all those who have not the law given to them, that they are delivered from that awful monster, [w]death and hell, and the devil, and the lake of fire and brimstone, which is endless torment; and they are restored to that God who gave them breath, which is the Holy One of Israel.

27. But wo unto him that has the law given, yea, that has all the commandments of God, like unto us, and that transgresseth them, and that wasteth the days of his probation, for awful is his state!

28. O that cunning plan of the evil one! O the vainness, and the frailties, and the foolishness of men! When they [z]are learned they think they are wise, and they hearken not unto the counsel of God, for they set it aside, supposing they know of themselves, wherefore, their wisdom is foolishness and it profiteth them not. And they shall perish.

29. But to be learned is good if they hearken unto the counsels of God.

30. But wo unto the rich, who are rich as to the things of the world. For because they are rich they despise the poor, and they persecute the meek, and their hearts are upon their treasures; wherefore, their treasure is their God. And behold, their treasure shall perish with them also.

31. And wo unto the deaf that will not hear; for they shall perish.

32. Wo unto the blind that will not see; for they shall perish also.

33. Wo unto the uncircumcised of heart, for a knowledge of their iniquities shall smite them at the last day.

34. Wo unto the liar, for he shall be thrust down to hell.

35. Wo unto the murderer who deliberately killeth, for he shall die.

36. Wo unto them who commit [y]whoredoms, for they shall be thrust down to hell.

37. Yea, wo unto those that worship idols, for the devil of all devils delighteth in them.

38. A, eia hoi, auwe ka poe a pau i make iloko o ko lakou
mau hewa; no ka mea, [z] e hoi hou no lakou i ke Akua la, a e ike
i kona maka, a e noho mau no iloko o ko lakou mau hala.
39. Ea, e na hoahanau i alohaia o'u, e hoomanao i ka weliweli
o ka hana ino ana i kela Akua Hemolele, a me ka weliweli no hoi
o ka ae wale ana aku i ka hoowalewale ana o kela mea maalea.
E hoomanao, o ka manao ma ke kino, he make ia, a o ka manao
ma ka uhane he ola mau loa ia.
40. E! e o'u mau hoahanau i alohaia, e haliu mai ka pepeiao
i ka'u olelo. E hoomanao i ka nani o ka Mea Hemolele o ka Iseraela. Mai olelo iho ua olelo aku la au i na mea paakiki e ku e ia oukou; no ka mea, ina paha e olelo oukou pela, e hoino no oukou i ka oiaio; no ka mea, ua olelo aku la au i na olelo a ko oukou Mea nana i hana. Ua ike au ua paakiki na olelo o ka oiaio e ku e ana i ka paumaele a pau; aka, aole ka poe pono i makau ia mau mea, no ka mea, e makemake ana lakou i ka oiaio, aole hoi i hoonaueueia.
41. E! e o'u mau hoahanau i alohaia, e hele mai i ka Haku,
ka Mea Hemolele. E hoomanao ua pololei kona mau aoao. Aia hoi, ua [2a] ololi ke ala no kanaka, aka ua moe ia me ka pololei imua ona, a o ka mea kiai puka oia ka Mea Hemolele o ka Iseraela; aole oia e hoonoho ana i kekahi kauwa malaila; aole hoi kekahi ala e ae, ma ka puka wale no, no ka mea, ua hiki ole ia ia ke hoopunipuniia; no ka mea, o ka Haku ke Akua kona inoa.
42. A o ka mea kikeke, e wehe no oia ia ia; a o ka poe [2b] naauao, a me ka poe i aoia, a o ka poe waiwai, i hoohaakeiia no ko lakou ike, a no ko lakou naauao, a no ko lakou waiwai; he oiaio, oia ka poe ana i hoowahawaha mai ai; a ke hoolei ole lakou i keia mau mea mai o lakou aku, a e manao lakou he poe naaupo lakou imua o ke Akua, a e hele mai me ka haahaa loa, aole oia e wehe no lakou.
43. Aka, e hunaia na mea o ka poe naauao a me ka poe akamai, mai o lakou aku no ka wa pau ole; he oiaio, o kela pomaikai i hoomakaukauia no ka poe hoano.
44. E na hoahanau i alohaia o'u, e hoomanao i ka'u mau olelo;
e nana mai, ke wehe nei au i ko'u mau aahu, a ke lulu nei au ia mau mea imua o oukou; ke pule nei au i ke Akua o ko'u ola e nana mai oia ia'u me kona maka ike lea; nolaila, e ike no oukou ma ka la mahope, i ka wa a na kanaka a pau e hookolokoloia'i no ka lakou mau hana, ua ike ke Akua o ka Iseraela ua lulu aku au i ka oukou mau hana ino mai ko'u uhane aku, a ke ku nei au me ka huali imua ona, a ua maemae au mai ko oukou koko mai.
45. E na hoahanau i alohaia o'u, e huli ae oukou mai ko oukou mau hewa ae; e lulu aku oukou i na kaula hao o ka mea e

38. And, in fine, wo unto all those who die in their sins; for they shall [z]return to God, and behold his face, and remain in their sins.

39. O, my beloved brethren, remember the awfulness in transgressing against that Holy God, and also the awfulness of yielding to the enticings of that cunning one. Remember, to be carnally-minded is death, and to be spiritually-minded is life eternal.

40. O, my beloved brethren, give ear to my words. Remember the greatness of the Holy One of Israel. Do not say that I have spoken hard things against you; for if ye do, ye will revile against the truth; for I have spoken the words of your Maker. I know that the words of truth are hard against all uncleanness; but the righteous fear them not, for they love the truth and are not shaken.

41. O then, my beloved brethren, come unto the Lord, the Holy One. Remember that his paths are righteous. Behold, the way for man is [2a]narrow, but it lieth in a straight course before him, and the keeper of the gate is the Holy One of Israel; and he employeth no servant there; and there is none other way save it be by the gate; for he cannot be deceived, for the Lord God is his name.

42. And whoso knocketh, to him will he open; and the [2b]wise, and the learned, and they that are rich, who are puffed up because of their learning, and their wisdom, and their riches—yea, they are they whom he despiseth; and save they shall cast these things away, and consider themselves fools before God, and come down in the depths of humility, he will not open unto them.

43. But the things of the wise and the prudent shall be hid from them forever—yea, that happiness which is prepared for the saints.

44. O, my beloved brethren, remember my words. Behold, I take off my garments, and I shake them before you; I pray the God of my salvation that he view me with his all-searching eye; wherefore, ye shall know at the last day, when all men shall be judged of their works, that the God of Israel did witness that I shook your iniquities from my soul, and that I stand with brightness before him, and am rid of your blood.

45. O, my beloved brethren, turn away from your sins; shake off the chains of him that would bind you fast; come unto that God who is the rock of your salvation.

makemake ana e nakinaki ia oukou a paa; e hele mai i ua Akua la, oia ka pohaku o ko oukou ola.

46. E hoomakaukau oukou i ko oukou mau uhane no kela la nani, i ka wa e haawiia mai ai ka uku pono i ka poe pono; oia ka la hookolokolo, i hopepe ole iho ai oukou me ka makau weliweli; i ole oukou e hoomanao i ko oukou hewa weliweli iwaena [2c]o ka hemolele, a e koiia e hooho aku, Hemolele, hemolele kou hoopai ana, e ka Haku ke Akua mana loa. Aka, ke ike nei au i kuu hewa, ua ae aku la au maluna o kou kanawai, a o ko'u lawehala ana no'u no ia, a ua [2d]loaa au i ke diabolo, i pio au i kona poino weliweli.

47. Aka hoi, e o'u mau hoahanau, he mea e pono ai anei e hoala aku au ia oukou i ka ike maopopo weliweli i keia mau mea? E hoowalania anei au i ko oukou mau uhane, ina i maemae ko oukou mau naau? E olelo maopopo aku anei au ia oukou, e like me ka maopopo ana o ka oiaio, ina ua maemae oukou mai ka hewa ae?

48. Aia hoi, ina ua hemolele oukou, e olelo au ia oukou no ka hemolele; aka, no ko oukou hemolele ole, a ke nana mai nei oukou ia'u me he kumu la, he mea pono ia'u ke ao aku ia oukou i ka hopena o ka hewa.

49. Aia hoi, ke hoopailua nei no ko'u uhane i ka hewa, a ke hauoli nei kuu naau i ka pono; a e hoolea no au i ka inoa hoano o ko'u Akua.

50. E hele mai, e o'u mau hoahanau, [2e]kela mea keia mea i makewai, e hele mai oukou i na wai; a o ka mea kala ole, e hele mai hoi e kuai no a e ai iho; oia, e hele mai e kuai i ka waina a me ka waiu me ke kala ole a me ke kumukuai ole.

51. Nolaila, mai hoomaunauna i ko oukou kala no ka mea lapuwale, i ka oukou hana hoi no ka mea i hoomaona ole. E hoolohe pono mai oukou ia'u, a e hoomanao i na olelo a'u i olelo aku ai, a e hele mai i ka Mea Hemolele o ka Iseraela, a e ai a maona i ka mea e make ole ana, aole hoi hiki ke hoopalahoia, a e olioli hoi ko oukou uhane ma ka momona.

52. Aia hoi, e na hoahanau o'u, e hoomanao i na olelo a ko oukou Akua; e pule mau ia ia ma ke ao, a e hoolea aku i kona inoa hoano ma ka po. E olioli ko oukou mau naau.

53. A e ike i ka nui o na berita a ka Haku, a me ka nui hoi o kona manao haahaa i na keiki a kanaka; a no kona nani, a me kona lokomaikai a aloha, ua olelo paa mai oia ia kakou [2f]aole e luku loa ia ka kakou poe hua, mamuli o ke kino, aka nana no e malama ia lakou; a ma na hanauna e aku, e lilo lakou i lala pono o ko ka hale o Iseraela.

54. Ano, e o'u mau hoahanau, ua makemake au e olelo hou aku ia oukou; ma ka la apopo e hai ai au ia oukou i ke koena o ka'u mau olelo. Amene.

46. Prepare your souls for that glorious day when justice shall be administered unto the righteous, even the day of judgment, that ye may not shrink with awful fear; that ye may not remember your awful guilt in [2c]perfectness, and be constrained to exclaim: Holy, holy are thy judgments, O Lord God Almighty—but I know my guilt; I transgressed thy law, and my transgressions are mine; and the devil hath [2d]obtained me, that I am a prey to his awful misery.

47. But behold, my brethren, is it expedient that I should awake you to an awful reality of these things? Would I harrow up your souls if your minds were pure? Would I be plain unto you according to the plainness of the truth if ye were freed from sin?

48. Behold, if ye were holy I would speak unto you of holiness; but as ye are not holy, and ye look upon me as a teacher, it must needs be expedient that I teach you the consequences of sin.

49. Behold, my soul abhorreth sin, and my heart delighteth in righteousness; and I will praise the holy name of my God.

50. Come, my brethren, [2e]every one that thirsteth, come ye to the waters; and he that hath no money, come buy and eat; yea, come buy wine and milk without money and without price.

51. Wherefore, do not spend money for that which is of no worth, nor your labor for that which cannot satisfy. Hearken diligently unto me, and remember the words which I have spoken; and come unto the Holy One of Israel, and feast upon that which perisheth not, neither can be corrupted, and let your soul delight in fatness.

52. Behold, my beloved brethren, remember the words of your God; pray unto him continually by day, and give thanks unto his holy name by night. Let your hearts rejoice.

53. And behold how great the covenants of the Lord, and how great his condescensions unto the children of men; and because of his greatness, and his grace and mercy, he has promised unto us that our seed shall [2f]not utterly be destroyed, according to the flesh, but that he would preserve them; and in future generations they shall become a righteous branch unto the house of Israel.

54. And now, my brethren, I would speak unto you more; but on the morrow I will declare unto you the remainder of my words. Amen.

20. Ano, e o'u mau hoahanau i alohaia, i ko kakou ike ana
ua haawi mai ko kakou Akua aloha i keia ike nui no keia mau
mea, e hoomanao kakou ia ia, a e waiho wale aku i ko kakou mau
hewa, aole hoi e kulou ko kakou mau poo, no ka mea, aole i hooleiia'ku kakou; aka hoi, ua kipakuia mai la kakou mailoko mai
o ko kakou aina hooilina; aka ua alakaiia mai la kakou i kahi
aina maikai ae; no ka mea, ua hana mai la ka Haku i ke kai i
alanui no kakou, a maluna no kakou o kahi mokupuni o ke kai.
21. Aka, nani na olelo hoopomaikai a ka Haku i ka poe e noho ana maluna o na [n]mokupuni o ke kai; nolaila, i kona i ana mai
i na mokupuni o ke kai, ke ike nei au aole o keia mokupuni wale
no, aka he nui ae; a e noho ana hoi na hoahanau o kakou maluna
o lakou.
22. No ka mea, ua [o]alakai ae la ka Haku ke Akua ia lakou,
ia manawa aku ia manawa aku, mai ko ka hale o Iseraela ae, e
like me kona manao a makemake. Ano, aia hoi, ke hoomanao
nei no ka Haku i ka poe a pau i haihaiia mai; nolaila, ke hoomanao nei oia ia kakou hoi.

11. A e hiki mai keia i kela la, e hohola hou mai ka Haku i
kona lima no ka lua o ka [l]manawa, e hoola i ke koena o kona poe
kanaka, i ka poe koe [m]mai Asuria mai, a mai Aigupita mai, a
mai Paterosa mai, a mai Kusa mai, a mai Elama mai, a mai Si-
nari mai, a mai Hamata mai, a mai na mokupuni mai o ke kai.
12. A e [n]kau no oia i hae no na lahuikanaka, a e hoiliili hoi i
ka [o]poe aea o ka Iseraela, a e [p]hoakoakoa mai i na mea puehu o
ka Iuda mai na kihi eha mai o ka honua.

2 NEPHI, 10

20. And now, my beloved brethren, seeing that our merciful God has given us so great knowledge concerning these things, let us remember him, and lay aside our sins, and not hang down our heads, for we are not cast off; nevertheless, we have been driven out of the land of our inheritance; but we have been led to a better land, for the Lord has made the sea our path, and we are upon an isle of the sea.

21. But great are the promises of the Lord unto them who are upon the [n]isles of the sea; wherefore as it says isles, there must needs be more than this, and they are inhabited also by our brethren.

22. For behold, the Lord God has [o]led away from time to time from the house of Israel, according to his will and pleasure. And now behold, the Lord remembereth all them who have been broken off, wherefore he remembereth us also.

2 NEPHI, 21

11. And it shall come to pass in that day that the Lord shall set his hand again [l]the second time to recover the remnant of his people which shall be left, [m]from Assyria, and from Egypt, and from Pathros, and from Cush, and from Elam, and from Shinar, and from Hamath, and from the islands of the sea.

12. And he shall [n]set up an ensign for the nations, and shall assemble the [o]outcasts of Israel, and [p]gather together the dispersed of Judah from the four corners of the earth.

3. A no ka ha ana'ku o na olelo a'u, e olelo aku no he nui o ka poe Genetile, He [f]baibala, he baibala, he baibala no ko makou, aole i hiki mai i baibala hou.

6. E ka mea [g]naaupo, e i mai auanei, He baibala, he baibala no ko makou, aole pono e loaa hou he baibala. Ua loaa anei ia oukou he baibala, ke ole ia ma o ka poe Iudaio la!

7. Aole anei oukou i ike he nui ae na lahuikanaka, aole hookahi wale no? Aole anei oukou i ike ua hana owau ka Haku ko oukou Akua, i na kanaka a pau, a ke hoomanao nei au i ka poe e noho ana maluna o na mokupuni o ke kai; a ke noho alii nei au ma na lani iluna, a ma ka honua ilalo; a ke hoopuka nei au i ka'u olelo i na keiki a kanaka, oiaio, maluna iho o na lahuikanaka a pau o ka honua?

8. Nolaila, no ke aha la oukou e ohumu nei, no ka loaa hou ana'e ka'u olelo ia oukou? Aole anei oukou i ike o ka olelo hoike a na lahuikanaka elua, he hoike ia ia oukou no'u, owau no ke Akua, a ke hoomanao nei no hoi au i kekahi lahui e like me kekahi? No ia mea, ke olelo nei au i na olelo like i kekahi lahui me kekahi. A ia laua e holo like ai, e [h]holo like no hoi ka laua hoike ana.

10. Nolaila, no ko oukou loaa ana he baibala, mai manao oukou eia iloko ona ka'u mau olelo a pau; mai manao hoi oukou ua kauoha ole au i na mea hou e palapalaia'i;

11. No ka mea, ke kauoha aku nei au i na kanaka a pau, ma ka hikina, a ma ke komohano, a ma ka akau, a ma ka hema, a ma na mokupuni o ke kai, e palapala lakou i na olelo a'u e olelo aku ai ia lakou; no ka mea, noloko mai o [i]na buke e palapalaia, e [j]hookolokolo no au i ko ke ao, i kela kanaka i keia kanaka e like me kana hana, e like me ka mea i palapalaia.

12. No ka mea, aia hoi, e olelo aku au i ka poe [k]Iudaio, a e kakau lakou ia mea; a e olelo aku no hoi au i ko [l]Nepai poe, a e kakau no lakou ia mea; a e olelo no hoi au i na ohana e ae o ka hale o Iseraela, a'u i alakai aku ai, a e kakau no lakou ia mea; a e [m]olelo aku au i na [n]lahuikanaka a pau o ka honua, a e kakau no lakou ia mea.

3. And because my words shall hiss forth—many of the Gentiles shall say: A [f]Bible! A Bible! We have got a Bible, and there cannot be any more Bible.

6. Thou [g]fool, that shall say: A Bible, we have got a Bible, and we need no more Bible. Have ye obtained a Bible save it were by the Jews?

7. Know ye not that there are more nations than one? Know ye not that I, the Lord your God, have created all men, and that I remember those who are upon the isles of the sea; and that I rule in the heavens above and in the earth beneath; and I bring forth my word unto the children of men, yea, even upon all the nations of the earth?

8. Wherefore murmur ye, because that ye shall receive more of my word? Know ye not that the testimony of two nations is a witness unto you that I am God, that I remember one nation like unto another? Wherefore, I speak the same words unto one nation like unto another. And when the two nations shall run together the testimony of the [h]two nations shall run together also.

10. Wherefore, because that ye have a Bible ye need not suppose that it contains all my words; neither need ye suppose that I have not caused more to be written.

11. For I command all men, both in the east and in the west, and in the north, and in the south, and in the islands of the sea, that they shall write the words which I speak unto them; for out of the [i]books which shall be written I will [j]judge the world, every man according to their works, according to that which is written.

12. For behold, I shall speak unto the [k]Jews and they shall write it; and I shall also speak unto the [l]Nephites and they shall write it; and I shall also [m]speak unto the other tribes of the house of Israel, which I have led away, and they shall write it; and I shall also speak unto [n]all nations of the earth and they shall write it.

MOKUNA 31.

1. Ano, ke hooki nei au, o Nepai, i ka'u wanana ana ia oukou, e o'u poe hoahanau i alohaia. A he mau mea kakaikahi
wale no ka'u i hiki ai ke palapala, a'u i ike ai e hiki io mai ana;
a he mau olelo kakaikahi wale no hoi, i hiki ia'u ke palapala o na
olelo a ko'u kaikaina o Iakoba.

2. Nolaila, ea, ua lawa ia'u na mea a'u i palapala'i, koe he
mau olelo kakaikahi na'u e olelo aku, no ke ao ana a Kristo; nolaila, e olelo aku au ia oukou me ka maopopo e like me ka maopopo o ka'u wanana ana.

3. No ka mea, ke hauoli nei ko'u naau iloko o [a] na mea maopopo; a mamuli o keia ano ke hana la ka Haku ke Akua mawaena o na keiki a kanaka. No ka mea, ke haawi mai nei ka Haku
ke Akua i malamalama i ka naau; no ka mea, ke olelo mai la oia
i na kanaka e like me ka lakou olelo, i ko lakou hoomaopopo ana.

4. Nolaila, ua makemake au e hoomanao oukou ua olelo aku
au ia oukou, no [b] kela kaula a ka Haku i hoike mai ai ia'u, ka
mea e bapetizo aku auanei i ke Keikihipa a ke Akua, o ka mea
nana e lawe aku i na hewa o ko ke ao nei.

5. Ano, ina he mea e pono ai no ke Keikihipa a ke Akua, a
he mea hemolele no hoi ia, ke bapetizoia me ka wai, e [c] malama ai i
ka pono a pau, ea, he nui aku keia mea e pono ai no kakou, he poe
hemolele ole, ke bapetizoia, he oiaio, me ka wai.

6. Ano, ke makemake nei au e niele ia oukou, e ko'u poe
hoahanau, ma ka mea hea i malama'i ke Keikihipa a ke Akua i
ka pono a pau, i kona bapetizoia'na me ka wai?

7. Aole anei oukou i ike ua hemolele ia? Aka me kona hemolele no, ke hoike mai la nae oia i na keiki a kanaka, e hoohaahaa ana oia ia ia iho ma ke kino imua o ka Makua, a e hoike ana
i ka Makua e hoolohe ana oia ia ia, ma ka malama ana i kona
mau kanawai;

8. Nolaila, mahope iho o kona bapetizoia'na me ka wai, iho
iho la ka Uhane Hemolele maluna ona ma ke [d] ano o kahi manu
nunu.

9. A, eia hou, e hoike mai ana keia mea i na keiki a kanaka
i ka ololi o ke ala, a me ka [e] pilikia o ka puka kahi e komo ai lakou, ua hana oia ia mea i kumu hoohalike imua o lakou.

10. A i aku la oia i na keiki a kanaka, E hahai mai oukou ia'u.

CHAPTER 31.

Nephi's predictions continued—Why the Savior would be baptized—The straight and narrow way.

1. And now I, Nephi, make an end of my prophesying unto you, my beloved brethren. And I cannot write but a few things, which I know must surely come to pass; neither can I write but a few of the words of my brother Jacob.
2. Wherefore, the things which I have written sufficeth me, save it be a few words which I must speak concerning the doctrine of Christ; wherefore, I shall speak unto you plainly, according to the plainness of my prophesying.
3. For my soul delighteth in [a]plainness; for after this manner doth the Lord God work among the children of men. For the Lord God giveth light unto the understanding; for he speaketh unto men according to their language, unto their understanding.
4. Wherefore, I would that ye should remember that I have spoken unto you concerning [b]that prophet which the Lord showed unto me, that should baptize the Lamb of God, which should take away the sins of the world.
5. And now, if the Lamb of God, he being holy, should have need to be baptized by water, to [c]fulfil all righteousness, O then, how much more need have we, being unholy, to be baptized, yea, even by water!
6. And now, I would ask of you, my beloved brethren, wherein the Lamb of God did fulfil all righteousness in being baptized by water?
7. Know ye not that he was holy? But notwithstanding he being holy, he showeth unto the children of men that, according to the flesh he humbleth himself before the Father, and witnesseth unto the Father that he would be obedient unto him in keeping his commandments.
8. Wherefore, after he was baptized with water the Holy Ghost descended upon him in the [d]form of a dove.
9. And again, it showeth unto the children of men the [e]straightness of the path, and the narrowness of the gate, by which they should enter, he having set the example before them.

Nolaila, e o'u poe hoahanau i alohaia, e hiki anei ia kakou ke hahai
ia Iesu, ke ae ole aku kakou e malama i na kauoha a ka Makua?
11. A i mai la ka Makua, E mihi oukou, e mihi oukou, a e
[f]bapetizoia ma ka inoa o ke Keiki punahele.
12. Aia hoi, hiki mai la no hoi ka leo o ke Keiki ia'u, i ka
i ana, O ka mea e bapetizoia ma ko'u inoa, ia ia e haawi mai ai ka
Makua i ka Uhane Hemolele, e like me au nei; no ia mea, e hahai
oukou ia'u, a e hana i na mea a oukou i ike mai ai ia'u e
hana ana.
13. Nolaila, e ko'u poe hoahanau i alohaia, ua ike au ina e
hahai oukou i ke Keiki, me ka manao ikaika o ka naau, e hana
ole ana i ka hookamani, aole hoi i ka hoopunipuni imua o ke
Akua, aka me ka manao oiaio, e mihi ana i ko oukou mau hala,
e hoike ana i ka Makua, e ae ana oukou e lawe maluna iho o oukou i ka inoa o Kristo, ma ka bapetizoia ana; oiaio, ma ka hahai
ana i ko oukou Haku a me ko oukou Mea e Ola'i ilalo iloko o ka
wai, e like me kana olelo; aia hoi, alaila e loaa'i ia oukou ka
Uhane Hemolele; oiaio, alaila e hiki mai ai ka bapetizo ana o ke
ahi a me ka Uhane Hemolele; alaila e hiki ai ia oukou ke olelo aku
me ka [g]olelo a na anela, a e hooho i ka hoolea ana i ka Mea
Hemolele o ka Iseraela.
14. Aka hoi, e ko'u poe hoahanau i alohaia, penei i hiki mai
ai ka leo o ke Keiki ia'u, i ka i ana, Mahope iho o ko oukou mihi
ana i ko oukou mau hala, a hoike ana aku i ka Makua e ae ana
oukou e malama i ka'u mau kauoha, ma ka bapetizo ana o ka
wai, a loaa ana ka bapetizo ana o ke ahi a me ka Uhane Hemolele, a i hiki ke olelo me ka olelo hou, oiaio, me ka olelo a na
anela, a mahope iho o keia ina e hoole mai ia'u, ua aho ia no
oukou, ina ua [h]ike ole oukou ia'u.
15. A lohe ae la au i kahi leo mai ka Makua mai, i ka i ana,
Oiaio, o na olelo a ko'u mea hiwahiwa ua oiaio a ua pololei. O
ka mea e hoomau ana a hiki i ka hopena, e hoolaia oia.
16. Ano, e o'u poe hoahanau i alohaia, ua ike au ma keia, i
ole e hoomau ke kanaka a hiki i ka hopena, i ka hahai ana i ke
kumu hoohalike o ke Keiki a ke Akua ola, aole e hiki ia ia ke
hoolaia.
17. Nolaila, e hana oukou i na mea a'u i hai aku ai ia oukou
a'u i ike ai, i na mea a ko oukou Haku, ka Mea Hoolapanai, e hana'i
auanei; no ka mea, no keia mea ua hoikeia mai la ia mau mea
ia'u, i ike ai oukou i ka [i]puka kahi a oukou e komo ai. No ka
mea, o ka puka kahi a oukou e komo ai, oia no ka mihi, a me ka
bapetizoia ana me ka wai; alaila e hiki mai ai ke kalaia'na o ko
oukou mau hala i ke ahi, a i ka Uhane Hemolele hoi.
18. Alaila aia oukou iloko o ke ala ololi a pololei e hiki aku ai
i ke ola mau loa; oiaio, ua komo oukou iloko ma ka puka; ua

10. And he said unto the children of men: Follow thou me. Wherefore, my beloved brethren, can we follow Jesus save we shall be willing to keep the commandments of the Father?

11. And the Father said: Repent ye, repent ye, and be [f]baptized in the name of my Beloved Son.

12. And also, the voice of the Son came unto me, saying: He that is baptized in my name, to him will the Father give the Holy Ghost, like unto me; wherefore, follow me, and do the things which ye have seen me do.

13. Wherefore, my beloved brethren, I know that if ye shall follow the Son, with full purpose of heart, acting no hypocrisy and no deception before God, but with real intent, repenting of your sins, witnessing unto the Father that ye are willing to take upon you the name of Christ, by baptism—yea, by following your Lord and your Savior down into the water, according to his word, behold, then shall ye receive the Holy Ghost; yea, then cometh the baptism of fire and of the Holy Ghost; and then can ye speak with the [g]tongue of angels, and shout praises unto the Holy One of Israel.

14. But, behold, my beloved brethren, thus came the voice of the Son unto me, saying: After ye have repented of your sins, and witnessed unto the Father that ye are willing to keep my commandments, by the baptism of water, and have received the baptism of fire and of the Holy Ghost, and can speak with a new tongue, yea, even with the tongue of angels, and after this should deny me, it would have been better for you that ye had not known me.

15. And I heard a voice from the Father, saying: Yea, the words of my Beloved are true and faithful. [h]He that endureth to the end, the same shall be saved.

16. And now, my beloved brethren, I know by this that unless a man shall endure to the end, in following the example of the Son of the living God, he cannot be saved

17. Wherefore, do the things which I have told you I have seen that your Lord and your Redeemer should do; for, for this cause have they been shown unto me, that ye might know the [i]gate by which ye should enter. For the gate by which ye should enter is repentance and baptism by water; and then cometh a remission of your sins by fire and by the Holy Ghost.

hana oukou e like me na kauoha a ka Makua a me ke Keiki; a ua loaa ia oukou ka Uhane Hemolele, ka mea e hoike ana no ka Makua a me ke Keiki, i ka hooko ana i ka olelo hoopomaikai ana i haawi mai ai, ina e komo oukou ma ke ala, e loaa'i ia oukou.

19. Ano, e na hoahanau i alohaia o'u, mahope iho o ko oukou komo ana iloko o keia ala pololei a ololi, ke ninau nei au, Ua pau anei ka hana? Aia hoi, ke i aku nei au ia oukou, aole; aole oukou i hiki i keia wahi, i ole ma o ka olelo la a Kristo, me ka manaoio naueue ole ia ia, e hilinai loa ana maluna iho o na hana maikai a ka Mea mana e ola'i;

20. Nolaila, e holo ikaika oukou e pono ai me ke kupaa iloko o Kristo, me ka nani loa o ka manaolana, a me ke aloha i ke Akua a i na kanaka a pau. Nolaila, ina e holo ikaika oukou e ahaaina ana ma na olelo a Kristo, a hoomau a hiki i ka hopena, aia hoi, wahi a ka Makua, E loaa ia oukou ke ola mau loa.

21. Ano, aia hoi, e na hoahanau i alohaia o'u, oia no ke [j] ala; aole kekahi ala e ae, aohe hoi kekahi inoa e ae i haawiia malalo iho o ka lani, i mea e ola'i ke kanaka iloko o ke aupuni o ke Akua. Ano, aia hoi, o ke ao ana a Kristo no keia, a oia wale no ke ao oiaio ana a ka Makua, a o ke Keiki, a o ka Uhane Hemolele, oia [k] hookahi Akua, me ka hopena ole. Amene.

---

2 NEPHI, 31

18. And then are ye in this straight and narrow path which leads to eternal life; yea, ye have entered in by the gate; ye have done according to the commandments of the Father and the Son; and ye have received the Holy Ghost, which witnesses of the Father and the Son, unto the fulfilling of the promise which he hath made, that if ye entered in by the way ye should receive.

19. And now, my beloved brethren, after ye have gotten into this straight and narrow path, I would ask if all is done? Behold, I say unto you, Nay; for ye have not come thus far save it were by the word of Christ with unshaken faith in him, relying wholly upon the merits of him who is mighty to save.

20. Wherefore, ye must press forward with a steadfastness in Christ, having a perfect brightness of hope, and a love of God and of all men. Wherefore, if ye shall press forward, feasting upon the word of Christ, and endure to the end, behold, thus saith the Father: Ye shall have eternal life.

21. And now, behold, my beloved brethren, this is the [j]way; and there is none other way nor name given under heaven whereby man can be saved in the kingdom of God. And now, behold, this is the doctrine of Christ, and the only and true doctrine of the Father, and of the Son, and of the Holy Ghost, which is [k]one God, without end. Amen.

KA BUKE A ENOSA.

MOKUNA 1.

1. Aia hoi, ua ike no au, o [a] Enosa i ko'u makuakane, he kanaka pono ia; no ka mea, ao mai la oia ia'u ma kana olelo iho, a ma ka hoopono a me ka hoonaauao o ka Haku. A e hoomaikai mau ia ka inoa o ko'u Akua no ia mea.
2. A e hai aku no au ia oukou no ka hakoko ana o'u imua o ke Akua, mamua o ka loaa ana ia'u ke kalaia o ko'u mau hala.
3. Aia hoi, hele aku la au e alualu aku i na holoholona hihiu ma ka ululaau; a o na olelo a'u i lohe pinepine ai i kuu makuakane e olelo ana no ke ola mau loa, a me ka hauoli o ka poe hoano, ua komo loa iloko o kuu naau.
4. A pololi ae la ko'u uhane; a kukuli iho la au ilalo imua o ko'u Mea nana i hana, a kahea aku la ia ia ma ka noi a me ka pule ikaika, no ko'u uhane iho; a pau loa ae la ka la ko'u hea ana ia ia; he oiaio, a hiki mai la ka po, e hookiekie mau ana au i ko'u leo iluna, i hiki ai ia i na lani.
5. A pae mai la kekahi leo ia'u, i ka i ana, E Enosa, ua kalaia'e la kou mau hala nou, a e pomaikai auanei oe.
6. A, ua ike au, o Enosa, ua hiki ole i ke Akua ke wahahee; nolaila, ua kahiliia'e la ko'u mau hewa.
7. A i aku la au, E ka Haku, pehea la ia i hanaia'i?
8. A i mai la ia ia'u, No kou manaoio ia Kristo, ka mea au i lohe ole e ai mamua, aole hoi i ike. A e hala ana na makahiki he nui loa mamua o kona hoike ana ia ia iho ma ke kino; nolaila, o hele aku, ua ola oe i kou manaoio.
9. Ano, eia kekahi, ia'u i lohe ai i keia mau olelo, hoomaka ae la ka makemake iloko o'u no ka pomaikai o ko'u poe hoahanau, o ko Nepai poe; nolaila, ninini aku la au i ko'u uhane a pau i ke Akua no lakou.
10. A oiai au e aumeume ana pela ma ka uhane, aia hoi, hiki hou mai la ka leo o ka Haku iloko o ko'u naau, i ka i ana, E hele no au i kou poe hoahanau, e like me ko lakou ikaika ma ka malama ana i ka'u mau kauoha. Ua [b] haawi aku au i keia aina ia lakou a he aina hoano ia; a e hoomainoino ole ana au ia ia, ke ole

THE BOOK OF ENOS

The Lord's promise concerning a Nephite record to come forth to the Lamanites—Character, condition, and wars of the two peoples.

1. Behold, it came to pass that
I, [a]Enos, knowing my father that
he was a just man—for he taught
me in his language, and also in
the nurture and admonition of
the Lord—and blessed be the
name of my God for it—
2. And I will tell you of the
wrestle which I had before God,
before I received a remission of
my sins.
3. Behold, I went to hunt beasts
in the forests; and the words
which I had often heard my father
speak concerning eternal
life, and the joy of the saints,
sunk deep into my heart.
4. And my soul hungered; and
I kneeled down before my Maker,
and I cried unto him in mighty
prayer and supplication for mine
own soul; and all the day long
did I cry unto him; yea, and
when the night came I did still
raise my voice high that it reached
the heavens.
5. And there came a voice
unto me, saying: Enos, thy sins
are forgiven thee, and thou shalt
be blessed.
6. And I, Enos, knew that God
could not lie; wherefore, my guilt
was swept away.
7. And I said: Lord, how is it
done?
8. And he said unto me: Because
of thy faith in Christ, whom
thou hast never before heard nor
seen. And many years pass away
before he shall manifest himself
in the flesh; wherefore, go to,
thy faith hath made thee whole.
9. Now, it came to pass that
when I had heard these words I
began to feel a desire for the welfare
of my brethren, the Nephites;
wherefore, I did pour out my
whole soul unto God for them.
10. And while I was thus struggling
in the spirit, behold, the
voice of the Lord came into my
mind again, saying: I will visit
thy brethren according to their
diligence in keeping my commandments.
I have [b]given unto
them this land, and it is a holy
land; and I curse it not save it be
for the cause of iniquity; wherefore,
I will visit thy brethren according
as I have said; and their
transgressions will I bring down
with sorrow upon their own heads.

no ka hana hewa; nolaila, e hele aku au i kou poe hoahanau me a'u i olelo aku ai; a e hoohaule au i ko lakou mau lawehala me ke kaumaha maluna o ko lakou mau poo iho.

11. A mahope iho o ko'u lohe ana i keia mau olelo, hoomaka ae la ka manaoio o'u e onipaa i ka Haku; a pule aku la au ia ia me na aumeume loihi no ko'u poe hoahanau, no ko Lamana poe.

12. Eia kekahi, mahope iho o ko'u pule, a hana ana me ka ikaika a pau, i mai la ka Haku ia'u, E ae aku au ia oe e like me kou makemake, no kou manaoio.

13. Ano hoi, eia no ka makemake a'u i makemake aku ai ia ia: Ina paha, e haule aku ko'u poe kanaka, ko Nepai poe, iloko o ka hewa, a ma o kekahi mea la e anaiia'i, a e anai ole ia ko Lamana poe, na ka Haku ke Akua [c]e malama i kekahi mooolelo o ko'u poe kanaka, o ko Nepai poe; ina paha ma o ka mana la o kona lima hemolele i hoopukaia'ku ai ia mea, ma kekahi la aku, i ko Lamana poe, i kaiia mai ai paha lakou i ke ola:

14. No ka mea, [d]ua makehewa ko makou hooikaika ana i keia manawa, e hoihoi hou ia lakou i ka manaoio. A hoohiki ae la lakou ma ko lakou huhu, ina he mea hiki, e hoopau loa lakou i ko makou mau mooolelo i kakauia, a me makou pu kekahi; a, i na mooolelo a pau no hoi o ko makou poe kupuna.

15. Nolaila, no ko'u ike ana ua hiki i ka Haku ke Akua ke [e]malama i ko makou mau mooolelo, kahea mau aku la au ia ia; no ka mea, ua i mai la oia ia'u, O ka mea au e noi mai ai ma ka manaoio, me ka paulele ana hoi e loaa ana ia oe ma ka inoa o Kristo, e loaa no ia ia oe.

16. A he manaoio ko'u, a kahea aku la au i ke Akua nana e malama i na mooolelo; a berita mai la oia ia'u, nana e [f]hoopuka aku ia mau mea i ko Lamana poe, i kona wa ku pono.

17, A ua ike au, o Enosa, e like auanei ia me ka berita ana i hana mai ai; nolaila, ua maha kuu uhane.

18. A i mai la ka Haku ia'u, Ua noi mai kou mau makua a me na kupuna hoi ia'u i keia mea; a e hanaia auanei ia mea ia lakou e like me ko lakou manaoio, no ka mea, ua like ko lakou manaoio me kou.

19. Eia kekahi, kaahele aku la au, o Enosa, iwaena o ka poe kanaka o Nepai, me ka wanana ana aku no na mea e hiki mai ana, a e hoike aku ana no na mea a'u i lohe ai a i ike ai hoi.

11. And after I, Enos, had heard these words, my faith began to be unshaken in the Lord; and I prayed unto him with many long strugglings for my brethren, the Lamanites.

12. And it came to pass that after I had prayed and labored with all diligence, the Lord said unto me: I will grant unto thee according to thy desires, because of thy faith.

13. And now behold, this was the desire which I desired of him —that if it should so be, that my people, the Nephites, should fall into transgression, and by any means be destroyed, and the Lamanites should not be destroyed, that the Lord God would [c]preserve a record of my people, the Nephites; even if it so be by the power of his holy arm, that it might be brought forth at some future day unto the Lamanites, that, perhaps, they might be brought unto salvation—

14. For at the present our strugglings were [d]vain in restoring them to the true faith. And they swore in their wrath that, if it were possible, they would destroy our records and us, and also all the traditions of our fathers.

15. Wherefore, I knowing that the Lord God was able to preserve our records, I cried unto him continually, for he had said unto me: Whatsoever thing ye shall ask in faith, believing that ye shall receive in the name of Christ, ye shall receive it.

16. And I had faith, and I did cry unto God that he would [e]preserve the records; and he covenanted with me that he would [f]bring them forth unto the Lamanites in his own due time.

17. And I, Enos, knew it would be according to the covenant which he had made; wherefore my soul did rest.

18. And the Lord said unto me: Thy fathers have also required of me this thing; and it shall be done unto them according to their faith; for their faith was like unto thine.

19. And now it came to pass that I, Enos, went about among the people of Nephi, prophesying of things to come, and testifying of the things which I had heard and seen.

26. Ano, me a'u i olelo aku ai no ka manaoio, aole ia he ike lea, pela no hoi me ka'u mau olelo nei. Aole e hiki ia oukou ke ike i ka oiaio o ia mau mea i kinohi, i ka ike lea ana, e like me ka manaoio aole ia he ike lea.

27. Aka, ina e ala oukou a e hooeueu ae i na mea ikaika o na naau o oukou, a hoao mai i ka'u mau olelo, a e hana me kekahi huna o ka manaoio; he oiaio, ina e hiki ia oukou ke makemake wale no e manaoio, e kuu aku i keia makemake e hana iloko o oukou, a hiki ia oukou ke manaoio ma ke ano kupono e hookaawale ae i wahi no kau wahi o ka'u mau olelo.

28. Ano, e hoohalike kakou i ka olelo i kekahi hua. Ano, ina e hookaawale ae oukou i wahi, e hiki ke kanuia kahi hua iloko o ko oukou mau naau, aia hoi, ina he hua oiaio, a he hua maikai, ina aole oukou e hoolei aku ia mea no ko oukou manaoio ole, i ku e ai oukou i ka Uhane o ka Haku, aia hoi, e hoomaka no ia e kupu ae iloko o ko oukou mau naau; a ia oukou e ike ai i keia kupu ana, e hoomaka no oukou e nalu iloko o oukou iho, he oiaio, he hua maikai neia, a oia hoi, ua maikai ka olelo, no ka mea, ke hoomaka nei ia e hooakea ae i kuu naau; he oiaio, ke hoomaka nei ia e hoomalamalama mai i kuu hoomaopopo ana; he oiaio, a ke hoomaka nei ia e lilo i ono loa ia'u.

29. Ano, aia hoi, aole anei e hoomahuahua keia i ko oukou manaoio? Ke i aku nei au ia oukou, ae; aole nae ia i ulu ae i ka ike lea.

30. Aka hoi, i ka omaka ana o ka hua, a i ka hoomaka ana e ulu, alaila, e pono no oukou ke olelo, ua maikai ka hua; no ka mea hoi, e pehu ana ia, a e omaka ana, a e hoomaka ana e ulu.

31. Ano, aia hoi, ua ike paka anei oukou he hua maikai keia? Ke i aku nei au ia oukou, ae; no ka mea, ke hua mai nei kela hua keia hua i kona ano like;

32. Nolaila, ina e ulu ana kekahi hua, he hua maikai ia, aka, ina e ulu ole ana ia, aia hoi, aole ia he maikai; nolaila, ua hooleiia'ku ia.

33. Ano, aia hoi, no ka hoao ana o oukou ia mea, a kanu iho la i ka hua, a e omaka ana, a e hoomaka ana e ulu, he mea e pono ai oukou ke ike ua maikai ka hua.

26. Now, as I said concerning faith—that it was not a perfect knowledge—even so it is with my words. Ye cannot know of their surety at first, unto perfection, any more than faith is a perfect knowledge.

27. But behold, if ye will awake and arouse your faculties, even to an experiment upon my words, and exercise a particle of faith, yea, even if ye can no more than desire to believe, let this desire work in you, even until ye believe in a manner that ye can give place for a portion of my words.

28. Now, we will compare the word unto a seed. Now, if ye give place, that a seed may be planted in your heart, behold, if it be a true seed, or a good seed, if ye do not cast it out by your unbelief, that ye will resist the Spirit of the Lord, behold, it will begin to swell within your breasts; and when you feel these swelling motions, ye will begin to say within yourselves—It must needs be that this is a good seed, or that the word is good, for it beginneth to enlarge my soul; yea, it beginneth to enlighten my understanding, yea, it beginneth to be delicious to me.

29. Now behold, would not this increase your faith? I say unto you, Yea; nevertheless it hath not grown up to a perfect knowledge.

30. But behold, as the seed swelleth, and sprouteth, and beginneth to grow, then you must needs say that the seed is good; for behold it swelleth, and sprouteth, and beginneth to grow.

31. And now, behold, are ye sure that this is a good seed? I say unto you, Yea; for every seed bringeth forth unto its own likeness.

32. Therefore, if a seed groweth it is good, but if it groweth not, behold it is not good, therefore it is cast away.

33. And now, behold, because ye have tried the experiment, and planted the seed, and it swelleth and sprouteth, and beginneth to grow, ye must needs know that the seed is good.

34. Ano, aia hoi, ua lawa anei ko oukou ike? Ae, ua lawa ko oukou ike ma ua mau mea la, a ua moe ko oukou manaoio; a o keia mea no ko oukou ike ana; no ka mea ua ike oukou ua hooakea mai ka olelo i ko oukou mau naau, a ua ike no hoi oukou ua omaka ae ia, a e hoomaka ana ko oukou hoomaopopo ana e hoomalamalamaia mai, a e hoomaka ana ko oukou mau naau e hooakeaia.

35. E! aole anei keia he oiaio? Ke i aku nei au ia oukou, ae; no ka mea, he malamalama ia; a o ka mea i malamalama he maikai ia, no ka mea, ua hiki ke ikeia; nolaila, he pono no oukou ke ike lea he maikai ia. Ano, aia hoi, mahope iho o ko oukou hoao ana i ua malamalama nei, ua lawa anei ko oukou ike?

36. Aia hoi, ke i aku nei au ia oukou, aole; aole no hoi oukou e waiho ae i ko oukou manaoio, no ka mea, ua hana me ko oukou manaoio wale no ma ke kanu ana i ka hua, e hiki ia oukou ke hoao aku, e ike ina he mea maikai ka hua.

37. A, aia hoi, i ka laau e hoomaka ai e ulu, e olelo no oukou, Ea, e malama pono loa kakou ia ia i komo ai kona aa, i ulu ai ia a e hoohua mai i ka hua ia kakou. Ano hoi, ina e malama pono loa oukou ia ia, e komo no kona aa, a e ulu ae, a e hoohua mai i ka hua.

38. Aka, ina e hoopalaleha oukou i ka laau, a manao ole i kona malamaia ana, aia hoi, aole no e komo na aa ona; a i ka wa e hiki mai ai ka wela o ka la a i hoowela mai ai ia ia, no ke aa ole ona, e mae ia, a e uhuki aku oukou ia ia, a hoolei aku iwaho.

39. Ano, aole keia no ka maikai ole o ka hua i kanuia; aole no hoi ia mea no ka maikai ole ana o ka hua ona i ohiia. Aka, no ka panoa o ko oukou lepo, a, no ko oukou malama ole ana i ka laau, nolaila, ua hiki ole ia oukou ke loaa ka hua ona.

40. A pela hoi, ina aole oukou e malama pono i ka olelo, e nana ana imua me ka maka o ka manaoio i ka hua ona, aole loa e hiki ia oukou ke ohi mai i ka hua o ka laau o ke ola.

41. Aka, ina e malama pono oukou i ka olelo, he oiaio, e malama pono i ka laau me ia i hoomaka ai e ulu, ma ko oukou manaoio me ka ikaika nui, a me ka hoomanawanui, e nana ana imua i ka hua ona, e komo no auanei na aa ona; a, aia hoi, e lilo no auanei ia i laau e ulu ana i ke ola mau loa;

42. A no ko oukou ikaika, a me ko oukou manaoio, a me ko oukou hoomanawanui me ka olelo me ka malama ana ia ia, i komo ai ilalo na aa ona iloko o oukou, aia hoi, mahope e ohi no oukou i ka hua ona, ka mea i maikai loa, a i ono loa hoi mamua o na mea ono a pau, a i keokeo loa mamua o na mea i keokeo a pau, he oiaio, a i maemae loa mamua o na mea i maemae a pau; a e ahaaina auanei oukou ma keia hua, a piha ae oukou, i pololi ole ai oukou, aole e makewai.

43. Alaila, e ko'u poe hoahanau, e ohi no oukou i na uku no ko oukou manaoio, me ko oukou ikaika, a ahonui, a hoomanawanui, e kali ana no ka laau e hoohua mai i ka hua no oukou.

34. And now, behold, is your knowledge perfect? Yea, your knowledge is perfect in that thing, and your faith is dormant; and this because ye know, for ye know that the word hath swelled your souls, and ye also know that it hath sprouted up, that your understanding doth begin to be enlightened, and your mind doth begin to expand.

35. O then, is not this real? I say unto you, Yea, because it is light; and whatsoever is light, is good, because it is discernible, therefore ye must know that it is good; and now behold, after ye have tasted this light is your knowledge perfect?

36. Behold I say unto you, Nay; neither must ye lay aside your faith, for ye have only exercised your faith to plant the seed that ye might try the experiment to know if the seed was good.

37. And behold, as the tree beginneth to grow, ye will say: Let us nourish it with great care, that it may get root, that it may grow up, and bring forth fruit unto us. And now behold, if ye nourish it with much care it will get root, and grow up, and bring forth fruit.

38. But if ye neglect the tree, and take no thought for its nourishment, behold it will not get any root; and when the heat of the sun cometh and scorcheth it, because it hath no root it withers away, and ye pluck it up and cast it out.

39. Now, this is not because the seed was not good, neither is it because the fruit thereof would not be desirable; but it is because your ground is barren, and ye will not nourish the tree, therefore ye cannot have the fruit thereof.

40. And thus, if ye will not nourish the word, looking forward with an eye of faith to the fruit thereof, ye can never pluck of the fruit of the tree of life.

41. But if ye will nourish the word, yea, nourish the tree as it beginneth to grow, by your faith with great diligence, and with patience, looking forward to the fruit thereof, it shall take root; and behold it shall be a tree springing up unto everlasting life.

42. And because of your diligence and your faith and your patience with the word in nourishing it, that it may take root in you, behold, by and by ye shall pluck the fruit thereof, which is most precious, which is sweet above all that is sweet, and which is white above all that is white, yea, and pure above all that is pure; and ye shall feast upon this fruit even until ye are filled, that ye hunger not, neither shall ye thirst.

43. Then, my brethren, ye shall reap the rewards of your faith, and your diligence, and patience, and long-suffering, waiting for the tree to bring forth fruit unto you.

30. Ano, e o'u poe hoahanau, ke makemake nei au mahope
iho o ko oukou loaa ana na hoike he nui wale me neia, me ka ike
hoi e hoike mai ana [u] na palapala hemolele no keia mau mea, e
hele mai oukou a e hoohua ae i ka hua i ka mihi;
31. He oiaio, ke makemake nei au e hele mai oukou a e hoopaakiki hou ole iho i ko oukou mau naau; no ka mea hoi, ano ka
manawa, a me ka la o ko oukou mau ola; a, nolaila, ina e mihi
oukou a hoopaakiki ole i ko oukou mau naau, e lawe koke ia mai ke
kumumanao nui hoolapanai ia oukou.
32. No ka mea, aia hoi, o keia ola ana oia no ka manawa no
na kanaka e hoomakaukau ai e halawai pu me ke Akua; he oiaio hoi, o ka la o keia ola ana oia no [v] ka la no na kanaka e hana
ai i na hana a lakou.
33. Ano, me a'u i olelo e ai ia oukou mamua, oiai ua loaa ia
oukou na hoike he nui wale me neia, nolaila, ke noi aku nei au
ia oukou, e hoopanee ole aku oukou i ko oukou la e mihi ai a hiki
i ka hopena; no ka mea, mahope iho o keia la o ke ola, i haawiia mai ai ia kakou e hoomakaukau ai no ke ao pau ole, aia hoi,
ina aole kakou e hoonui ae i ko kakou manawa oiai ma keia ola
ana, alaila, e hiki mai ai ka po o ka pouli, iloko olaila e hiki ole
ai ka hana ke hanaia.
34. Aole e hiki ia oukou ke olelo, ia oukou e laweia mai ai i
keia manawa pilikia weliweli, E mihi no au, e hoi no au i ko'u Akua.
Aole, aole loa e hiki ia oukou ke olelo ae i keia; no ka mea, o
kela uhane hookahi nana i noho ma ko oukou kino i ka manawa
a oukou e puka aku ai mai keia ola ana'ku, na ua uhane hookahi
la auanei ka mana e noho ma ko oukou kino ma kela ao mau loa.
35. No ka mea, aia hoi, ina ua hoopanee ae oukou i ko oukou
la e mihi ai, a hiki wale aku i ka make, aia hoi, ua lilo ae oukou
malalo iho o ka uhane o ke diabolo, a e hoopaa ana oia ia oukou
nona; no ia mea, ua haalele iho ka Uhane o ka Haku ia oukou,
aohe ona kuleana iloko o oukou, a no ke diabolo ka [w] mana a pau
maluna iho o oukou; a oia no ka noho hope ana o ka poe hewa.

4. A eia kekahi, ma ka makahiki kanakolukumamahiku o ke
au o na lunakanawai, haele aku la he huakai he nui loa, elima
tausani eha haneri kanaka, me ka lakou poe wahine a me ka lakou poe keiki, mai ka [d] aina aku o Zarahemela iloko o ka [e] aina
ma ka akau.
5. A eia kekahi, o Hagota, he kanaka akamai loa oia, nolaila,
hele aku la oia a kapili iho la nona i [f] kekahi moku nui, ma na
palena o ka [g] aina Momona, ma ka [h] aina o Neoneo, a hoolana
aku la ia mea iloko o ke kai homohana, ma ka [i] puali ololi i hiki
aku ai i ka [j] aina akau.
6. A, aia hoi, he nui na mea o ko Nepai poe i komo aku iloko,
a holo aku la me ka ai a nui, a me na wahine a me na keiki he
nui no hoi; a holo aku la lakou me ka ihu i ka akau. A pela i
pau ai ka makahiki kanakolukumamahiku.

ALMA, 34

30. And now, my brethren, I would that, after ye have received so many witnesses, seeing that the holy [u]scriptures testify of these things, ye come forth and bring fruit unto repentance.

31. Yea, I would that ye would come forth and harden not your hearts any longer; for behold, now is the time and the day of your salvation; and therefore, if ye will repent and harden not your hearts, immediately shall the great plan of redemption be brought about unto you.

32. For behold, this life is the time for men to prepare to meet God; yea, behold the day of this life is the [v]day for men to perform their labors.

33. And now, as I said unto you before, as ye have had so many witnesses, therefore, I beseech of you that ye do not procrastinate the day of your repentance until the end; for after this day of life, which is given us to prepare for eternity, behold, if we do not improve our time while in this life, then cometh the night of darkness wherein there can be no labor performed.

34. Ye cannot say, when ye are brought to that awful crisis, that I will repent, that I will return to my God. Nay, ye cannot say this; for that same spirit which doth possess your bodies at the time that ye go out of this life, that same spirit will have power to possess your body in that eternal world.

35. For behold, if ye have procrastinated the day of your repentance even until death, behold, ye have become subjected to the spirit of the devil, and he doth seal you his; therefore, the Spirit of the Lord hath withdrawn from you, and hath no place in you, and the devil hath [w]all power over you; and this is the final state of the wicked.

ALMA, 63

4. And it came to pass that in the ‡thirty and seventh year of the reign of the judges, there was a large company of men, even to the amount of five thousand and four hundred men, with their wives and their children, departed out of the [d]land of Zarahemla into the land which was [e]northward.

5. And it came to pass that Hagoth, he being an exceedingly curious man, therefore he went forth and built him an [f]exceedingly large ship, on the borders of the [g]land Bountiful, by the [h]land Desolation, and launched it forth into the west sea, by the [i]narrow neck which led into the [j]land northward.

6. And behold, there were many of the Nephites who did enter therein and did sail forth with much provisions, and also many women and children; and they took their course northward. And thus ended the thirty and seventh year.

7. A i ka makahiki kanakolukumamawalu, kapili ae la ua kanaka nei i [k]na moku e ae. A hoi mai la no hoi ka moku mua, a he nui wale na kanaka i komo hou iloko ona; a lawe pu no hoi lakou i ka ai a nui, a holo hou aku la i ka aina akau.

8. A eia kekahi, aole kekahi mea i lohe hou ia no lakou. A ke manao nei makou ua poho iho la lakou iloko o ka hohonu o ke kai. A eia kekahi, holo aku la hookahi moku hou no hoi; a kahi ona i holo aku ai, aole makou i ike.

9. A eia kekahi, ma ua makahiki nei, he nui na kanaka i hele aku iloko o ka aina akau. A pela i pau ai ka makahiki kanakolukumamawalu.

Hoike o Iesu Kristo ia ia iho i ka poe kanaka o Nepai, i ka wa a na kanaka i akoakoa ai ma kahi hookahi ma ka aina Momona, a lawelawe mai la ia lakou; a ma keia ano oia i hoike aku ai ia lakou.

MOKUNA 11.

1. Ano, eia kekahi, ua akoakoa na kanaka he lehulehu ma kahi hookahi, o ka poe kanaka o Nepai, a puni ka [a]luakini ma ka [b]aina o Momona; a e haohao ana a e kahaha ana kekahi me kekahi, a e hoike ana kekahi i kekahi i ka [c]loli kupanaha nui i hiki mai ai;

2. A e kamailio ana no hoi lakou no keia Iesu Kristo, ka mea nona ka [d]hoailona i haawiia mai no kona make.

3. A eia kekahi, oiai lakou e kamailio ana pela kekahi me kekahi, lohe ae la lakou i kekahi leo, me he mea la ua pae mai la ia mailoko mai o ka lani; a alawa ae la lakou i ko lakou mau maka i o a ia nei, no ka mea, hoomaopopo ole lakou i ka leo a lakou i lohe ai; a, aole ia he leo kalakala, aole hoi he leo nui; aka hoi, [e]he leo uuku ia, hou mai la nae ia i ka poe i lohe, iwaena konu, a, aole kekahi wahi o ko lakou kino i hoohaalulu ole ia e ia; he oiaio, hou mai la ia ia lakou iloko loa, a hoowela mai la i na naau o lakou.

4. A eia kekahi, lohe hou aku la lakou i ka leo, a hoomaopopo ole lakou ia mea;

5. A lohe hou aku la lakou i ke kolu o ka manawa i ka leo, a hoohakahaka aku la i ko lakou mau pepeiao e lohe ia mea; a malaila na maka o lakou i kahi o ke kupinai; a haka pono aku la i ka lani, kahi o ka leo i pae mai ai;

6. A, aia hoi, i ke kolu o ka manawa hoomaopopo aku la lakou i ka leo a lakou i lohe ai; a i mai la ia ia lakou:

ALMA, 63

7. And in the thirty and eighth
year, this man built [k]other ships.
And the first ship did also return,
and many more people did enter
into it; and they also took much
provisions, and set out again to
the land northward.
8. And it came to pass that
they were never heard of more.
And we suppose that they were
drowned in the depths of the sea.
And it came to pass that one other
ship also did sail forth; and
whither she did go we know not.
9. And it came to pass that in
this year there were many people
who went forth into the land
northward. And thus ended the
thirty and eighth year.

3 NEPHI, 11

Jesus Christ did show himself unto the people of Nephi, as the multitude were gathered together in the land Bountiful, and did minister unto them; and on this wise did he show himself unto them.

Comprising chapters 11 to 26 inclusive.

CHAPTER 11.

The Eternal Father proclaims the Christ—The Resurrected Christ appears—The multitude permitted to feel his wounds—Mode of baptism prescribed—Contention and disputation forbidden—Christ the rock.

1. And now it came to pass
that there were a great multitude
gathered together, of the
people of Nephi, round about the
[a]temple which was in the [b]land
Bountiful; and they were marveling
and wondering one with
another, and were showing one
to another the [c]great and marvelous
change which had taken
place.
2. And they were also conversing
about this Jesus Christ,
of whom the [d]sign had been
given concerning his death.
3. And it came to pass that
while they were thus conversing
one with another, they heard a
voice as if it came out of heaven;
and they cast their eyes round
about, for they understood not
the voice which they heard; and
it was not a harsh voice, neither
was it a loud voice; nevertheless,
and notwithstanding it being a
[e]small voice it did pierce them
that did hear to the center, insomuch
that there was no part of
their frame that it did not cause
to quake; yea, it did pierce them
to the very soul, and did cause
their hearts to burn.
4. And it came to pass that
again they heard the voice, and
they understood it not.
5. And again the third time
they did hear the voice, and did
open their ears to hear it; and
their eyes were towards the
sound thereof; and they did look
steadfastly towards heaven, from
whence the sound came.
6. And behold, the third time
they did understand the voice
which they heard; and it said
unto them:

7. E nana mai i ka'u Keiki punahele, iloko ona a'u i olioli loa ai, iloko ona a'u i [f]hoonani ai i ko'u inoa, e hoolohe oukou ia ia.

8. A eia kekahi, ia lakou i hoomaopopo ai, leha hou ae la lakou i ko lakou mau maka i ka lani; a, aia hoi, ike aku la lakou i kekahi [g]kanaka e iho mai ana mailoko mai o ka lani; a ua hoaahuia oia i ka aahu keokeo, a iho iho la ia a ku iho la mawaena konu o lakou, a alawa ae la na maka o na kanaka a pau ia ia, a aa ole lakou e oaka ae i na waha o lakou, aole hoi kekahi i kekahi, a ike ole iho la i ke ano o ia mea, no ka mea, manao iho la lakou he anela ia i ikea e lakou.

9. A eia kekahi, hohola mai la ia i kona lima, a olelo mai la i na kanaka, i ka i ana:

10. Aia hoi, owau no o Iesu Kristo, ka mea a ka poe kaula i hoike aku ai e hele mai ana i ke ao nei;

11. A, aia hoi, [h]owau no ka malamalama a me ke ola o ke ao nei; a ua inu iho la au noloko o kela [i]apu awaawa a ka Makua i haawi mai ai ia'u, a ua [j]hoonani aku i ka Makua ma ka lawe ana maluna iho o'u i [k]na hala o ko ke ao nei, a ma ia mea wau i ae aku ai i ka makemake o ka Makua ma na mea a pau, mai kinohi mai.

12. A eia kekahi, ia Iesu i olelo mai ai i ua mau olelo nei, hina iho la ka poe kanaka a pau i ka honua, no ka mea, hoomanao iho la lakou ua [l]wananaia mawaena o lakou, e hoike ana o Kristo ia ia iho ia lakou mahope iho o kona pii ana i ka lani.

13. A eia kekahi, olelo mai la ka Haku ia lakou, i ka i ana:

14. E ala, a e hele mai io'u nei, e hiki ia oukou ke [m]hou mai i ko oukou mau lima iloko o ko'u aoao, a e hiki no hoi ia oukou ke haha mai i na wahi o na kui ma ko'u mau lima, a ma ko'u mau wawae, i ike oukou owau no ke Akua o ka Iseraela, a o [n]ke Akua o ko ka honua a pau, a ua pepehiia mai a make no [o]na hala o ko ke ao nei.

15. A eia kekahi, hele aku la na kanaka, a [p]hou aku la i ko lakou mau lima iloko o kona aoao, a haha aku la i na wahi o na kui ma kona mau lima, a ma kona mau wawae; a o keia ka lakou i hana'i, e hele pakahi ana, a hiki i ka wa a lakou a pau i hele aku ai, a ike aku la me ko lakou mau maka iho, a haha aku la me ko lakou mau lima, a ike oiaio iho la a hoike aku la, oia no ia, ka mea i palapalaia mai ai e ka [q]poe kaula e hele mai ana.

16. A ia lakou a pau i hele aku ai a ike aku ai no lakou iho, hea ae la lakou me ka lokahi o ka manao, i ka i ana:

17. Hosana! E hoomaikaiia'ku ka inoa o ke [r]Akua Kiekie Loa! A hina iho la lakou ma na wawae o Iesu, a hoomana aku la ia ia.

7. Behold my Beloved Son, in whom I am well pleased, in whom I [f]have glorified my name —hear ye him.

8. And it came to pass, as they understood they cast their eyes up again towards heaven; and behold, they saw a [g]Man descending out of heaven; and he was clothed in a white robe; and he came down and stood in the midst of them; and the eyes of the whole multitude were turned upon him, and they durst not open their mouths, even one to another, and wist not what it meant, for they thought it was an angel that had appeared unto them.

9. And it came to pass that he stretched forth his hand and spake unto the people, saying:

10. Behold, I am Jesus Christ, whom the prophets testified shall come into the world.

11. And behold, [h]I am the light and the life of the world; and I have drunk out of that [i]bitter cup which the Father hath given me, and have [j]glorified the Father in taking upon me the [k]sins of the world, in the which I have suffered the will of the Father in all things from the beginning.

12. And it came to pass that when Jesus had spoken these words the whole multitude fell to the earth; for they remembered that it had been [l]prophesied among them that Christ should show himself unto them after his ascension into heaven.

13. And it came to pass that the Lord spake unto them saying:

14. Arise and come forth unto me, that ye may [m]thrust your hands into my side, and also that ye may feel the prints of the nails in my hands and in my feet, that ye may know that I am the God of Israel, and the [n]God of the whole earth, and have been slain for the [o]sins of the world.

15. And it came to pass that the multitude went forth, and [p]thrust their hands into his side, and did feel the prints of the nails in his hands and in his feet; and this they did do, going forth one by one until they had all gone forth, and did see with their eyes and did feel with their hands, and did know of a surety and did bear record, that it was he, of whom it was written by the [q]prophets, that should come.

16. And when they had all gone forth and had witnessed for themselves, they did cry out with one accord, saying:

17. Hosanna! Blessed be the name of the [r]Most High God! And they did fall down at the feet of Jesus, and did worship him.

18. A eia kekahi, olelo mai la oia ia Nepai, (no ka mea, aia no o [s]Nepai mawaena o na kanaka,) a kauoha mai la oia ia ia e hele ae.

19. A ala ae la o Nepai a hele aku la, a kulou iho la oia imua o ka Haku, a [t]honi aku la i kona mau wawae.

20. A kauoha mai la ka Haku ia ia, e ala'e oia. A ala ae la ia a ku iho la imua ona.

21. A i mai la ka Haku ia ia, Ke haawi aku nei au ia oe i ka [u]mana e [v]bapetizo aku i keia poe kanaka, i ka wa a'u e [w]pii hou ai i ka lani.

22. A hea hou mai la ka Haku i na mea e ae, a i mai la no hoi ia lakou pela; a haawi mai la oia ia lakou i ka [x]mana e bapetizo aku. A i mai la oia ia lakou: Ma keia ano oukou e bapetizo aku ai; [y]aole hoi na hoopaapaa mawaena o oukou.

23. He oiaio ka'u e olelo aku nei ia oukou, o ka mea e mihi ana i kona mau hewa ma o ka oukou mau olelo la, a makemake mai e bapetizoia ma kuu inoa, ma keia ano e bapetizo aku ai ia ia, aia hoi, e iho ilalo kekahi o oukou me ia a e [z]ku iloko o ka wai, a ma kuu inoa e bapetizo aku ai ia ia.

24. Ano hoi, eia na olelo e olelo aku ai, e hea ana ia ia ma ka inoa, i ka i ana:

25. Mamuli o ka [2a]mana i haawiia mai ia'u e Iesu Kristo, [2b]ke bapetizo aku nei au ia oe iloko o ka inoa o ka Makua, a o ke Keiki, a o ka Uhane Hemolele. Amene.

26. Alaila e hookomo iho ia ia iloko o ka wai, a e puka hou mai mailoko mai o ka wai.

27. A mamuli o keia ano oukou e bapetizo aku ai ma ko'u inoa, no ka mea hoi, he oiaio ka'u e olelo aku nei ia oukou, o ka [2c]Makua, a me ke Keiki, a me ka Uhane Hemolele, hookahi no lakou; a [2d]owau no iloko o ka Makua, a o ka Makua iloko o'u, a o ka Makua me a'u nei, ua [2e]hookahi maua.

28. A e like me ka'u i kauoha aku ai ia oukou, [2f]pela oukou e bapetizo aku ai. A [2g]aole hoi na hoopaapaa ana mawaena o oukou, e like me ia mamua aku nei; aole hoi na hoopaapaa ana mawaena o oukou no na mea nui o ko'u ao ana, e like me ia mamua aku nei;

29. No ka mea, oiaio, he oiaio ka'u e olelo aku nei ia oukou, o ka mea ia ia ka [2h]uhane paio, aole no'u nei ia, aka no ke diabolo, oia no ka makua o ka paio, a ke hooeueu la oia i na naau o na kanaka e paio me ka huhu, kekahi me kekahi.

30. Aia hoi, aole keia ko'u ao ana, e hooeueu aku i na naau o na keiki a kanaka me ka huhu, kekahi e ku e i kekahi; aka eia ko'u ao ana, e [2i]hoopauia'ku na mea e like me ia.

18. And it came to pass that he spake unto Nephi (for [s]Nephi was among the multitude) and he commanded him that he should come forth.

19. And Nephi arose and went forth, and bowed himself before the Lord and did [t]kiss his feet.

20. And the Lord commanded him that he should arise. And he arose and stood before him.

21. And the Lord said unto him: I give unto you [u]power that ye shall [v]baptize this people when I am [w]again ascended into heaven.

22. And again the Lord called others, and said unto them likewise: and he gave unto them [x]power to baptize. And he said unto them: On this wise shall ye baptize; and there shall be [y]no disputations among you.

23. Verily I say unto you, that whoso repenteth of his sins through your words and desireth to be baptized in my name, on this wise shall ye baptize them—Behold, ye shall go down and [z]stand in the water, and in my name shall ye baptize them.

24. And now behold, these are the words which ye shall say, calling them by name, saying:

25. Having [2a]authority given me of Jesus Christ, [2b]I baptize you in the name of the Father, and of the Son, and of the Holy Ghost. Amen.

26. And then shall ye immerse them in the water, and come forth again out of the water.

27. And after this manner shall ye baptize in my name; for behold, verily I say unto you, [2c]that the Father, and the Son, and the Holy Ghost are one; [2d]and I am in the Father, and the Father in me, and the Father and I are [2e]one.

28. And according as I have commanded you [2f]thus shall ye baptize. And there shall be [2g]no disputations among you, as there have hitherto been; neither shall there be disputations among you concerning the points of my doctrine, as there have hitherto been.

29. For verily, verily I say unto you, he that hath the spirit of [2h]contention is not of me, but is of the devil, who is the father of contention, and he stirreth up the hearts of men to contend with anger, one with another.

30. Behold, this is not my doctrine, to stir up the hearts of men with anger, one against another; but this is my doctrine, that [2i]such things should be done away.

31. Aia hoi, oiaio, he oiaio ka'u e olelo aku nei ia oukou, e
hai aku no au ia oukou i kuu ao ana.
32. A eia kuu ao ana, a o ke ao ana ia a ka Makua i haawi
mai ai ia'u; a ke [2j]hoike aku nei au no ka Makua, a ke hoike mai
la ka Makua no'u, a ke hoike mai nei ka Uhane Hemolele no ka
Makua a me a'u, a ke hoike aku nei au e kauoha ana ka Makua
i na kanaka a pau, ma kela wahi keia wahi, e mihi a e manaoio
mai ia'u;
33. A o ka mea i manaoio mai ia'u, a i [2k]bapetizoia'ku, e hoolaia auanei oia; a o lakou no ka poe e loaa'i ke aupuni o ke
Akua.
34. A o ka mea i manaoio ole mai ia'u, a i bapetizo ole ia'ku,
e hoohewaia auanei oia.
35. Oiaio, he oiaio ka'u e olelo aku nei ia oukou, o keia no
ko'u ao ana; a ke [2l]hoike aku nei au no ia mea mai ka Makua
mai; a o ka mea e [2m]manaoio ana ia'u, e manaoio ana oia i ka
Makua no hoi; a e [2n]hoike aku no ka Makua ia ia no'u; no ka
mea, e hoalauna oia ia ia [2o]me ke ahi a me ka Uhane Hemolele;
36. A pela ka Makua e [2p]hoike aku ai no'u; a e hoike aku no
ka Uhane Hemolele ia ia no ka Makua a me au; no ka mea, o
ka [2q]Makua, a me au nei, a me ka Uhane Hemolele, hookahi
makou.
37. A ke i hou aku nei au ia oukou, e mihi oukou e pono ai,
a e lilo me he keiki uuku la, a e [2r]bapetizoia'ku ma ko'u inoa, a i
ole ia, aole loa e hiki ia oukou ke loaa keia mau mea.
38. A ke i hou aku nei au ia oukou e mihi oukou e pono ai, a
e bapetizoia'ku ma ko'u inoa, a e lilo me he [2s]keiki uuku la, a i ole
ia, aole loa e hiki ia oukou ke loaa ke aupuni o ke Akua.
39. Oiaio, he oiaio ka'u e olelo aku nei ia oukou, o keia no
ko'u ao ana; a o ka mea e kukulu ana maluna o keia mea, e kukulu ana oia maluna iho o ko'u pohaku; a e [2t]lanakila ole na
ipuka o ka po maluna ona.
40. A o ka mea e hai aku ana i ka mea i oi aku, a i ole, i ka
mea i emi mai i keia, a e hookupaa aku ia mea no ko'u ao ana, no
ka ino mai ia, a ua kukulu ole ia maluna iho o ko'u pohaku, aka
e kukulu ana oia maluna iho o ke [2u]kahua one, a e hamama ana
na ipuka o ka po e loaa ka mea o ia ano, i ka wa e hiki mai ai ka
wai, a e nou mai ai ka makani maluna iho ona.
41. Nolaila, e hele aku i keia poe kanaka, a e hai aku i na
olelo a'u i olelo aku ai, i ko na welau o ka honua.

31. Behold, verily, verily, I say unto you, I will declare unto you my doctrine.

32. And this is my doctrine, and it is the doctrine which the Father hath given unto me; [2j]and I bear record of the Father, and the Father beareth record of me, and the Holy Ghost beareth record of the Father and me; and I bear record that the Father commandeth all men, everywhere, to repent and believe in me.

33. And whoso believeth in me, and is [2k]baptized, the same shall be saved; and they are they who shall inherit the kingdom of God.

34. And whoso believeth not in me, and is not baptized, shall be damned.

35. Verily, verily, I say unto you, that this is my doctrine, [2l]and I bear record of it from the Father; and [2m]whoso believeth in me believeth in the Father also; and unto him will the Father [2n]bear record of me, for he will visit him [2o]with fire and with the Holy Ghost.

36. And thus will the Father [2p]bear record of me, and the Holy Ghost will bear record unto him of the Father and me; [2q]for the Father, and I, and the Holy Ghost are one.

37. And again I say unto you, ye must repent, and become as a little child, and be [2r]baptized in my name, or ye can in nowise receive these things.

38. And again I say unto you, ye must repent, and be baptized in my name, and become as a [2s]little child, or ye can in nowise inherit the kingdom of God.

39. Verily, verily, I say unto you, that this is my doctrine, and whoso buildeth upon this buildeth upon my rock, and [2t]the gates of hell shall not prevail against them.

40. And whoso shall declare more or less than this, and establish it for my doctrine, the same cometh of evil, and is not built upon my rock; but he buildeth upon a [2u]sandy foundation, and the gates of hell stand open to receive such when the floods come and the winds beat upon them.

41. Therefore, go forth unto this people, and declare the words which I have spoken, unto the ends of the earth.

MOKUNA 12. *(E nana ia Mataio 5.)*

1. A eia kekahi, ia Iesu i olelo mai ai i ua mau olelo nei ia [a]Nepai, a i ka poe i heaia, (ano, he [b]umikumamalua ka nui o ka poe i heaia, a i loaa ka [c]mana a me ka oihana e bapetizo,) a, aia hoi, hohola mai la oia i kona lima i na kanaka, a hea mai la ia lakou, i ka i ana: Pomaikai oukou, ke hoolohe mai oukou i na olelo a ua poe umikumamalua nei, a'u i wae aku ai maiwaena mai o oukou e lawelawe aku ia oukou, a e lilo i poe kauwa na oukou; a ia lakou wau i [d]haawi aku ai i ka mana, i bapetizo aku ai lakou ia oukou me ka wai, a mahope iho o ko oukou bapetizoia ana me ka wai, aia hoi, e bapetizo aku au ia oukou [e]me ke ahi a me ka Uhane Hemolele; nolaila, pomaikai oukou, ina e manaoio mai oukou ia'u, a e bapetizoia'ku, mahope iho o ko oukou nana ana ia'u, a ike ana ke ola nei wau.

2. A eia hou, pomaikai loa lakou ka poe e manaoio mai ana ma ka oukou mau olelo, no ko oukou hoike ana ua nana mai oukou ia'u, a ua ike oukou ke ola nei owau. He oiaio, pomaikai ka poe e manaoio auanei i ka oukou mau olelo, a e iho ilalo iloko o na hohonu o ka haahaa, a e [f]bapetizoia; no ka mea, e hoolaunaia'ku auanei lakou [g]me ke ahi a me ka Uhane Hemolele, a e loaa auanei ke kalaia'na o ko lakou mau hala.

3. He oiaio, pomaikai ka poe i [h]haahaa ma ka uhane, ka poe i hele mai io'u nei, no ka mea, no lakou ke aupuni o ka lani.

4. A eia hou, pomaikai ka poe a pau e u ana, no ka mea, e hooluoluia'ku lakou;

5. A pomaikai ka poe akahai, no ka mea, e lilo auanei ka honua ia lakou.

6. A pomaikai ka poe a pau i pololi a makewai no ka pono; no ka mea, e [i]hoomaonaia lakou me ka Uhane Hemolele.

7. A pomaikai ka poe i aloha aku, no ka mea, e alohaia mai lakou.

8. A pomaikai ka poe a pau i maemae ma ka naau, no ka mea, e ike lakou i ke Akua.

9. A pomaikai ka poe uwao a pau, no ka mea, e iia'e lakou he poe keiki na ke Akua.

10. A pomaikai ka poe a pau i [j]hana ino ia mai no ko'u inoa, no ka mea, no lakou ke aupuni o ka lani.

11. A e pomaikai ana no oukou, ke hoino mai na kanaka ia oukou, a e hoomaau mai hoi, a no'u nei e olelo wahahee mai ai ia oukou i na mea ino a pau,

12. No ka mea, e loaa ia oukou ka [k]hauoli nui a e olioli nui hoi, no ka mea, he nui ka uku no oukou ma ka lani; pela lakou i hoomaau aku ai i ka poe kaula mamua o oukou.

CHAPTER 12.

The Savior's teachings to the Nephites—He calls and commissions the twelve disciples—His words to the multitude—The Sermon on the Mount retold—Compare Matthew 5.

1. And it came to pass that
when Jesus had spoken these
words unto [a]Nephi, and to those
who had been called, (now the
number of them who had been
called, and received [b]power and
authority to baptize, was [c]twelve)
and behold, he stretched forth his
hand unto the multitude, and
cried unto them, saying: Blessed
are ye if ye shall give heed unto
the words of these twelve whom
I have chosen from among you to
minister unto you, and to be your
servants; and unto them I have
[d]given power that they may baptize you with water: and after
that ye are baptized with water,
behold, I will baptize you [e]with
fire and with the Holy Ghost;
therefore blessed are ye if ye
shall believe in me and be baptized, after that ye have seen
me and know that I am.
2. And again, more blessed
are they who shall believe in
your words because that ye shall
testify that ye have seen me, and
that ye know that I am. Yea,
blessed are they who shall believe in your words, and come
down into the depths of humility
and be [f]baptized, for they shall
be visited [g]with fire and with the
Holy Ghost, and shall receive a
remission of their sins.
3. Yea, blessed are the [h]poor
in spirit who come unto me, for
theirs is the kingdom of heaven.
4. And again, blessed are all
they that mourn, for they shall
be comforted.
5. And blessed are the meek,
for they shall inherit the earth.
6. And blessed are all they
who do hunger and thirst after
righteousness, for they shall be
[i]filled with the Holy Ghost.
7. And blessed are the merciful, for they shall obtain mercy.
8. And blessed are all the pure
in heart, for they shall see God.
9. And blessed are all the
peacemakers, for they shall be
called the children of God.
10. And blessed are all they
who are [j]persecuted for my
name's sake, for theirs is the
kingdom of heaven.
11. And blessed are ye when
men shall revile you and persecute, and shall say all manner of
evil against you falsely, for my
sake;
12. For ye shall have [k]great
joy and be exceeding glad, for
great shall be your reward in
heaven; for so persecuted they
the prophets who were before
you.

13. Oiaio, he oiaio ka'u e olelo aku nei ia oukou, ke haawi aku nei au ia oukou e lilo i paakai no ka honua; aka, ina e pau auanei ka liu o ka paakai, [l]pehea la e liuia'i ka honua? Aohe o ka paakai mea e pono ai ma ia hope, e kiola wale ia iwaho, a e hehiia malalo iho o na wawae o na kanaka.

14. Oiaio, he oiaio ka'u e olelo aku nei ia oukou, ke haawi aku nei au ia oukou e lilo i malamalama o keia poe kanaka. O ke kulanakauhale i ku ma kahi kiekie aole ia e nalowale.

15. Aia hoi, ke hoa aku nei anei na kanaka i ke kukui a waiho aku ia mea malalo iho o ke poi? Aole, aka ma kahi e kau ai o ke kukui, a e haawi ana ia i ka malamalama i ka poe a pau iloko o ka hale;

16. Nolaila, e hoakaka aku oukou i ko oukou malamalama imua o keia poe kanaka, i ike mai ai lakou i ka oukou hana maikai ana, a i hoonani aku ai i ko oukou Makua i ka lani.

17. Mai manao oukou i hele mai nei au e hoopau i ke kanawai a me ka ka poe kaula. Aole au i hele mai nei e hoopau, aka e hooko;

18. No ka mea, he oiaio ka'u e olelo aku nei ia oukou, [m]aole i lilo aku kahi huna aole hoi kahi lihi iki mai ke kanawai ae, aka iloko o'u ua hookoia mai ia mea a pau.

19. Aia hoi, ua haawi aku au ia oukou i ke kanawai a me na kauoha a ko'u Makua, i manaoio mai ai oukou ia'u, a i mihi ai oukou i ko oukou mau hewa, a hele mai io'u nei me ka [n]naau pepe a me ka uhane akahai. Aia hoi, ia oukou na kauoha imua o oukou, [o]a ua ko iho la no ke kanawai;

20. Nolaila, e hele mai oukou io'u nei, a e hoolaia'ku oukou; no ka mea, he oiaio ka'u e olelo aku nei ia oukou, ina aole oukou e malama i ka'u [p]mau kauoha, a'u i kauoha aku ai ia oukou i keia manawa, aole loa oukou e komo mai iloko o ke aupuni o ka lani.

21. Ua lohe oukou ua oleloia mai e ka poe o ka wa kahiko, a ua palapalaia no hoi imua o oukou, Mai pepehi kanaka oe; a o ka mea e pepehi i ke kanaka, e lilo ana ia i ka [q]hoohewaia e ke Akua.

22. Aka, eia ka'u e olelo aku nei ia oukou, o ka mea e huhu aku i kona hoahanau, e lilo ana ia i kona [r]hoohewa ana. O ka mea e olelo ae i kona hoahanau, E, Raka, e lilo ia i mea no ka aha hookolokolo; a o ka mea e olelo aku, E, ka lapuwale, e lilo ia i mea no ke ahi o gehena;

23. Nolaila, ina e hele mai oukou io'u nei, a [s]e makemake paha e hele mai io'u nei, a i manao he mea ka kou hoahanau e ku e ia oe,

24. E hele aku i kou hoahanau la, a e hoolaulea mua ia i kou

13. Verily, verily, I say unto you, I give unto you to be the salt of the earth; but if the salt shall lose its savor wherewith [l]shall the earth be salted? The salt shall be thenceforth good for nothing, but to be cast out and to be trodden under foot of men.

14. Verily, verily, I say unto you, I give unto you to be the light of this people. A city that is set on a hill cannot be hid.

15. Behold, do men light a candle and put it under a bushel? Nay, but on a candlestick, and it giveth light to all that are in the house;

16. Therefore let your light so shine before this people, that they may see your good works and glorify your Father who is in heaven.

17. Think not that I am come to destroy the law or the prophets. I am not come to destroy but to fulfil;

18. For verily I say unto you, one jot nor one tittle [m]hath not passed away from the law, but in me it hath all been fulfilled.

19. And behold, I have given you the law and the commandments of my Father, that ye shall believe in me, and that ye shall repent of your sins, and come unto me with a [n]broken heart and a contrite spirit. Behold, ye have the commandments before you, and the [o]law is fulfilled.

20. Therefore come unto me and be ye saved; for verily I say unto you, that except ye shall keep my [p]commandments, which I have commanded you at this time, ye shall in no case enter into the kingdom of heaven.

21. Ye have heard that it hath been said by them of old time, and it is also written before you, that thou shalt not kill, and whosoever shall kill shall be in danger of the [q]judgment of God;

22. But I say unto you, that whosoever is angry with his brother shall be in danger of [r]his judgment. And whosoever shall say to his brother, Raca, shall be in danger of the council; and whosoever shall say, Thou fool, shall be in danger of hell fire.

23. Therefore, if ye shall come unto me, or shall [s]desire to come unto me, and rememberest that thy brother hath aught against thee—

hoahanau, alaila, e hele mai io'u nei me ka manao ikaika o ka naau, a na'u oukou e hookipa aku.

25. E hoolaulea koke aku oe i kou hoa ku e, oiai oe me ia ma ke alanui, o hopu aku oia ia oe i kekahi manawa, a e hooleiia'ku oe iloko o ka halepaahao.

26. Oiaio, he oiaio ka'u e olelo aku nei ia oe, aole loa oe e puka e mai iwaho olaila, a pau ae la ka 'senine hope i ka ukuia e oe. A oiai oe iloko o ka halepaahao, e hiki anei ia oe ke uku aku i hookahi senine? Oiaio, he oiaio ka'u e olelo aku nei ia oukou, aole.

27. Aia hoi, ua palapalaia e ka poe o ka wa kahiko, Mai moekolohe oe:

28. Aka, eia ka'u e olelo aku nei ia oukou, o ka mea e nana ana i ka wahine, e kuko hewa aku ia ia, ua moekolohe no oia ia manawa ma kona naau.

29. Aia hoi, ke haawi aku nei au i kauoha ia oukou, i "ae ole aku oukou i kekahi o ua mau mea nei e komo iloko o ko oukou naau;

30. No ka mea, e aho no oukou e hoole ia oukou iho i keia mau mea, ma na mea a oukou e hapai ai i ko oukou kea, mamua o ko oukou hooleiia'na iloko o gehena.

31. Ua palapalaia, o ka mea hoohemo i kana wahine, e haawi aku oia nana i ka palapala no ka hemo ana.

32. Oiaio, he oiaio ka'u e olelo aku nei ia oukou, o ka mea e "hoohemo wale i kana wahine, ke ole ia no ka foranikationa, nana no ia e hoomoekolohe aku; a o ka mea e mare i ua wahine hemo la, ua moekolohe no ia.

33. A eia hou i palapalaia, Mai hoohiki wahahee oe, aka, e hooko aku oe no ka Haku i kau mea i hoohiki ai.

34. Aka oiaio, he oiaio ka'u e olelo aku nei ia oukou, mai hoohiki iki; aole ma ka lani, no ka mea, o ko ke Akua noho alii ia;

35. Aole hoi ma ka honua, no ka mea, o kona keehana wawae ia;

36. Aole hoi oe e hoohiki ma ke poo, no ka mea, aole e hiki ia oe ke hoolilo i kekahi oho i eleele, aole hoi i keokeo;

37. Aka, penei ka oukou kamailio ana o ka ae, he ae ia; o ka ole, he ole ia; no ka mea, o ka mea i oi aku i keia, he ino ia.

38. Aia hoi, ua palapalaia, He maka no ka maka, a he niho no ka niho.

39. Aka, eia ka'u e olelo aku nei ia oukou, mai hoopai aku oe i ka ino, aka o ka mea nana oe e papai mai ma kou papalina akau, e haliu aku oe ia ia ma kekahi.

40. A ina e kahihi wale aku kekahi kanaka ia oe ma ke kanawai, a e lawe i kou kapa komo, e ho hou aku no hoi ia ia i kou aahu.

24. Go thy way unto thy brother, and first be reconciled to thy brother, and then come unto me with full purpose of heart, and I will receive you.

25. Agree with thine adversary quickly while thou art in the way with him, lest at any time he shall get thee, and thou shalt be cast into prison.

26. Verily, verily, I say unto thee, thou shalt by no means come out thence until thou hast paid the uttermost [t]senine. And while ye are in prison can ye pay even one senine? Verily, verily, I say unto you, Nay.

27. Behold, it is written by them of old time, that thou shalt not commit adultery;

28. But I say unto you, that whosoever looketh on a woman, to lust after her, hath committed adultery already in his heart.

29. Behold, I give unto you a commandment, that ye suffer [u]none of these things to enter into your heart;

30. For it is better that ye should deny yourselves of these things, wherein ye will take up your cross, than that ye should be cast into hell.

31. It hath been written, that whosoever shall put away his wife, let him give her a writing of divorcement.

32. Verily, verily, I say unto you, that whosoever [v]shall put away his wife, saving for the cause of fornication, causeth her to commit adultery; and whoso shall marry her who is divorced committeth adultery.

33. And again it is written, thou shalt not forswear thyself, but shalt perform unto the Lord thine oaths;

34. But verily, verily, I say unto you, swear not at all; neither by heaven, for it is God's throne;

35. Nor by the earth, for it is his footstool;

36. Neither shalt thou swear by the head, because thou canst not make one hair black or white;

37. But let your communication be Yea, yea; Nay, nay; for whatsoever cometh of more than these is evil.

38. And behold, it is written, an eye for an eye, and a tooth for a tooth;

39. But I say unto you, that ye shall not resist evil, but whosoever shall smite thee on thy right cheek, turn to him the other also;

40. And if any man will sue thee at the law and take away thy coat, let him have thy cloak also;

41. A o ka mea e koi mai ia oe e hele i hookahi mile, e hele pu me ia i elua.
42. O ka mea e noi mai ia oe, e haawi aku nana, a o ka mea e noi e lawe lilo ole i kau mea, mai kaii ae oe.
43. Aia ua palapalaia no hoi, E aloha aku i kou hoalauna, a e inaina aku i kou enemi;
44. Aka hoi, eia ka'u e olelo aku nei ia oukou, e aloha aku i ko oukou poe enemi, e hoomaikai aku hoi i ka poe kuamuamu mai ia oukou, e hana lokomaikai aku hoi i ka poe inaina mai ia oukou, a e pule aku hoi i ka poe e hana ino mai ia oukou, a hoomaau mai ia oukou;
45. I lilo ai oukou i poe keiki na ko oukou Makua i ka lani; no ka mea, nana no i hoopuka mai i kona la maluna o ka poe ino a me ka poe maikai;
46. Nolaila, o ua mau mea la o ka wa kahiko, na mea malalo iho o ke kanawai iloko o'u, ua ko a pau loa.
47. Ua hoopauia'ku na mea kahiko, a ua lilo na mea a pau i hou;
48. Nolaila, ke makemake nei au i hemolele oukou e like me au nei, a me ka hemolele o ko oukou Makua ma ka lani.

21. A he oiaio ka'u e olelo aku nei ia oukou, o oukou no ka poe a'u i olelo aku ai, He poe hipa e ae no ka'u, aole no keia pa; he pono hoi no'u e alakai mai ia lakou, a e lohe auanei lakou i ko'u leo; a hookahi auanei pa hipa, a me ke kahuhipa hookahi hoi.

MOKUNA 17.

1. Aia hoi, i ka wa a Iesu i olelo mai ai i ua mau olelo nei, alawa hou ae la oia i o ia nei maluna o na kanaka, a olelo mai la ia lakou, aia hoi, ua kokoke mai kuu manawa.

3 NEPHI, 12

41. And whosoever shall compel thee to go a mile, go with him twain.
42. Give to him that asketh thee, and from him that would borrow of thee turn thou not away.
43. And behold it is written also, that thou shalt love thy neighbor and hate thine enemy;
44. But behold I say unto you, love your enemies, bless them that curse you, do good to them that hate you, and pray for them who despitefully use you and persecute you;
45. That ye may be the children of your Father who is in heaven; for he maketh his sun to rise on the evil and on the good.
46. Therefore those things which were of old time, which were under the law, in me are [w]all fulfilled.
47. Old things [x]are done away, and all things have become new.
48. Therefore I would that ye should be perfect even [y]as I, or your Father who is in heaven is perfect.

3 NEPHI, 15

21. And verily I say unto you, that [s]ye are they of whom I said: Other sheep I have which are not of this fold; them also I must bring, and they shall hear my voice; and there shall be one fold, and one shepherd.

3 NEPHI, 17

CHAPTER 17.

The Savior's instructions continued—The lost tribes—The Savior heals the sick and blesses little children—A marvelous and touching scene.

1. Behold, now it came to pass that when Jesus had spoken these words he looked round about again on the multitude, and he said unto them: Behold, my time is at hand.

2. Ke ike nei au ua nawaliwali oukou, ua hiki ole ia oukou
ke hoomaopopo mai i ka'u mau olelo a pau i kauohaia mai ai au,
e ka Makua, e olelo aku ia oukou i keia manawa;
3. Nolaila, e hele oukou i ko oukou mau wahi, a e hoomanao
iho i na mea a'u i olelo aku ai, a e noi aku i ka Makua, ma ko'u
inoa, i hiki ia oukou ke hoomaopopo; a e hoomakaukau i ko oukou mau naau no ka la apopo, a e hele hou mai au io oukou la.
4. Aka, e [a]hele ana au ano i ka Makua la, a e hoike aku ana
no hoi ia'u iho i [b]na ohana nalowale o ka Iseraela, no ka mea, aole
lakou i nalowale i ka Makua, no ka mea, ua ike oia i kahi ana i
lawe aku ai ia lakou.
5. A eia kekahi, ia Iesu i olelo mai ai pela, alawa hou ae la
oia i kona mau maka i o ia nei maluna o na kanaka, a ike aku la
ua kahe ka waimaka o lakou, a haka pono ae la lakou ia ia, me
he mea la e noi aku ana lakou ia ia e noho iki hou me lakou.
6. A i aku la oia ia lakou: Aia hoi, ua piha ka naau o'u me
ke aloha aku ia oukou;
7. [c]Ina he poe mai mawaena o oukou, e lawe mai ia lakou ia
nei. Ina he poe oopa, makapo, hapakue, mumuku, lepera, a me
ka poe lolo, a kuli, a me ka poe i hoehaia ma kela ano keia ano,
e lawe mai ia lakou ia nei, a e hoola aku au ia lakou, no ka mea,
he aloha ko'u no oukou; ua piha ka naau o'u me ka lokomaikai;
8. No ka mea, ke ike nei au e makemake ana oukou, e hoike
aku au ia oukou i ka mea a'u i hana aku ai i ko oukou poe hoahanau ma Ierusalema, no ka mea, ke ike nei au [d]ua lawa ko oukou manaoio, e hoola aku ai au ia oukou.
9. A eia kekahi, ia ia i olelo mai ai pela, hele lokahi aku la
na kanaka a pau, me ko lakou poe mai, a me ko lakou poe i hoehaia, a me ko lakou poe oopa, a me ko lakou poe makapo, a me
ko lakou poe aa, a me ka poe a pau i hoehaia ma kela ano keia
ano; a [e]hoola mai la oia ia lakou, i kela mea keia mea i ka laweia'na o lakou io na la;
10. A kulou iho la lakou a pau, o ka poe i hoolaia, a me ka
poe ola no hoi, ma kona mau wawae, a hoomana aku la ia ia; a
[f]honi iho la ka poe a pau i hiki no ka paapu o na kanaka, i kona
mau wawae, a hoauau iho la i kona mau wawae me ko lakou
waimaka.
11. A eia kekahi, kauoha mai la oia e laweia'ku ka lakou poe
keiki uuku.
12. [g]A lawe ae la lakou i ka lakou poe keiki uuku, a hoonoho
iho la ia lakou ilalo ma ka honua a puni ia, a ku iho la o Iesu
iwaena konu; a emi ihope na kanaka a laweia ae la lakou a pau
io na la.
13. A eia kekahi, ia lakou a pau i laweia'ku ai, a ku iho la no

2. I perceive that ye are weak, that ye cannot understand all my words which I am commanded of the Father to speak unto you at this time.

3. Therefore, go ye unto your homes, and ponder upon the things which I have said, and ask of the Father, in my name, that ye may understand, and prepare your minds for the morrow, and I come unto you again.

4. But now I [a]go unto the Father, and also to show myself unto the [b]lost tribes of Israel, for they are not lost unto the Father, for he knoweth whither he hath taken them.

5. And it came to pass that when Jesus had thus spoken, he cast his eyes round about again on the multitude, and beheld they were in tears, and did look steadfastly upon him as if they would ask him to tarry a little longer with them.

6. And he said unto them: Behold, my bowels are filled with compassion towards you.

7. [c]Have ye any that are sick among you? Bring them hither. Have ye any that are lame, or blind, or halt, or maimed, or leprous, or that are withered, or that are deaf, or that are afflicted in any manner? Bring them hither and I will heal them, for I have compassion upon you; my bowels are filled with mercy.

8. For I perceive that ye desire that I should show unto you what I have done unto your brethren at Jerusalem, for I see that your faith is [d]sufficient that I should heal you.

9. And it came to pass that when he had thus spoken, all the multitude, with one accord, did go forth with their sick and their afflicted, and their lame, and with their blind, and with their dumb, and with all them that were afflicted in any manner; and he did [e]heal them every one as they were brought forth unto him.

10. And they did all, both they who had been healed and they who were whole, bow down at his feet, and did worship him; and as many as could come for the multitude did [f]kiss his feet, insomuch that they did bathe his feet with their tears.

11. And it came to pass that he commanded that their [g]little children should be brought.

12. So they brought their little children and set them down upon the ground round about him, and Jesus stood in the midst; and the multitude gave way till they had all been brought unto him.

13. And it came to pass that when they had all been brought, and Jesus stood in the midst, he commanded the multitude that they should [h]kneel down upon the ground.

o Iesu mawaena konu, kauoha mai la oia i na kanaka e [h]kukuli iho ilalo ma ka honua.

14. A eia kekahi, ia lakou i kukuli iho ai ilalo ma ka honua, uhu iho la o Iesu iloko ona iho a i aku la: E ka Makua, ua [i]pilikia mai au no ka hewa o ka poe kanaka o ka hale o Iseraela.

15. A ia ia i olelo mai ai i ua mau olelo nei, [j]kukuli iho la no hoi oia ma ka honua; a, aia hoi, pule aku la oia i ka Makua, a o na mea ana i pule aku ai, ua hiki ole ke palapalaia, a hoike ae la na kanaka, ka poe i lohe ia ia.

16. A mamuli o keia ano lakou i hoike aku ai: [k]Aole i ike iki ka maka, aole hoi i lohe ka pepeiao, mamua, i na mea nui a kupanaha e like me ka makou i ike ai a i lohe ai ia Iesu i olelo aku ai i ka Makua;

17. Aole e hiki i kekahi alelo ke olelo, aole no hoi e hiki ke palapalaia e kekahi kanaka, aole hoi e hiki i na naau o na kanaka ke hoomaopopo i na mea nui a kupanaha, e like me ka makou i ike ai a i lohe ai no hoi ia Iesu e olelo ana; a ua hiki ole no hoi i kekahi mea ke hoomaopopo i ka olioli i hoopiha mai ai i ko makou mau naau, i ka manawa a makou i lohe ai ia ia e pule ana no makou i ka Makua.

18. A eia kekahi, ia Iesu i hoopau ai i ka pule ana i ka Makua, ala ae la ia; aka, no ka olioli nui o na kanaka, ua ilihia lakou.

19. A eia kekahi, olelo mai la o Iesu ia lakou, a kena mai la ia lakou e ala'e.

20. A ala ae la lakou mai ka honua ae, a i mai la oia ia lakou: Pomaikai oukou no ko oukou manaoio. Ano hoi, o kuu olioli ua piha.

21. A ia ia i olelo mai ai i keia mau olelo, uwe iho la ia, a hoike ae la na kanaka no ia mea, a [l]lawe pakahi ae la oia i ka lakou poe keiki, a hoopomaikai iho la ia lakou, a pule aku la i ka Makua no lakou.

22. A ia ia i hana'i i keia, uwe hou iho la oia,

23. A olelo mai la ia i na kanaka, a i mai la ia lakou: E nana i ka oukou poe uuku.

24. A ia lakou i nana aku ai e ike, leha ae la lakou i ko lakou mau maka i ka lani, a ike aku la lakou i na lani e hamama ana, a ike aku la lakou i na anela e iho mai ana mailoko mai o ka lani me he mea la, [m]mawaena o ke ahi;

25. A iho mai la lakou ilalo a hoopuni ae la i ua poe uuku la a puni, a ua hoopuniia lakou me ke ahi; a lawelawe ae la ka poe anela ia lakou, a ike a lohe a hoike ae la na kanaka; a ua ike lakou ua oiaio ko lakou hoike ana, no ka mea, lohe aku la a ike aku la lakou a pau, o kela kanaka keia kanaka nona iho; a elua tausani a me na haneri elima paha ka nui o lakou; a he poe kane, wahine a me na kamalii lakou.

14. And it came to pass that when they had knelt upon the ground, Jesus groaned within himself, and said: Father, I am [i]troubled because of the wickedness of the people of the house of Israel.

15. And when he had said these words, he himself also [j]knelt upon the earth; and behold he prayed unto the Father, and the things which he prayed cannot be written, and the multitude did bear record who heard him.

16. And after this manner do they bear record: [k]The eye hath never seen, neither hath the ear heard, before, so great and marvelous things as we saw and heard Jesus speak unto the Father;

17. And no tongue can speak, neither can there be written by any man, neither can the hearts of men conceive so great and marvelous things as we both saw and heard Jesus speak; and no one can conceive of the joy which filled our souls at the time we heard him pray for us unto the Father.

18. And it came to pass that when Jesus had made an end of praying unto the Father, he arose; but so great was the joy of the multitude that they were overcome.

19. And it came to pass that Jesus spake unto them, and bade them arise.

20. And they arose from the earth, and he said unto them: Blessed are ye because of your faith. And now behold, my joy is full.

21. And when he had said these words, he wept, and the multitude bare record of it, and [l]he took their little children, one by one, and blessed them, and prayed unto the Father for them.

22. And when he had done this he wept again;

23. And he spake unto the multitude, and said unto them: Behold your little ones.

24. And as they looked to behold they cast their eyes towards heaven, and they saw the heavens open, and they saw angels descending out of heaven as it were in the midst of fire; and they came down and encircled those little ones about, and they [m]were encircled about with fire; and the angels did minister unto them.

25. And the multitude did see and hear and bear record; and they know that their record is true for they all of them did see and hear, every man for himself; and they were in number about two thousand and five hundred souls; and they did consist of men, women, and children.

19. Nolaila, ea, e pule mau oukou e pono ai i ka Makua ma
ko'u inoa;
20. A o ka mea a oukou e noi aku ai i ka Makua ma ko'u
inoa, a ua pono, me ka manaoio e loaa ia oukou, aia hoi, e haawiia
mai ia ia oukou.
21. [n] E pule mau oukou ma na ohana o oukou i ka Makua ma
ko'u inoa, e hoopomaikaiia mai ka oukou poe wahine a me ka oukou poe keiki.
22. A, aia hoi, e halawai pinepine oukou i kahi hookahi, a,
mai papa aku i kekahi kanaka i ka hele ana io oukou la, i ka wa
a oukou e halawai ai i kahi hookahi, aka e ae aku oukou ia lakou
e hele mai io oukou la, a e papa ole aku ia lakou;
23. Aka, e pule oukou no lakou, a e hoolei ole aku ia lakou
mawaho; a ina paha e hele pinepine mai lakou io oukou la, alaila, e pule aku oukou i ka Makua, ma ko'u inoa, no lakou;
24. Nolaila, e hapai ae oukou i ko oukou malamalama iluna
i alohi aku ai ia i ko ke ao nei. Aia hoi, owau no ka [o] malamalama a oukou e hapai aku ai iluna—i ka mea a oukou i ike mai ai
i hanaia e au. Aia hoi, ke ike nei oukou ua pule aku la au i ka
Makua, a ua ike oukou a pau;

MOKUNA 27.

1. A eia kekahi, i ka wa e hele ana ka [a] poe haumana a Iesu
a e hai ana i na mea a lakou i lohe ai a i ike ai hoi, a e bapetizo
ana ma ka inoa o Iesu, hiki mai keia, ua houluuluia mai ka poe
haumana i kahi hookahi, a ua huiia ma ka [b] pule ikaika a me ka
[c] hookeai.
2. A hoike hou mai la o Iesu ia ia iho ia lakou, no ka mea, e
pule ana lakou i ka Makua, ma kona inoa; a hele mai la o Iesu a
ku iho la mawaena konu o lakou, a olelo mai la ia lakou: Heaha
ka oukou makemake a'u e haawi aku ai ia oukou;
3. A i aku la lakou ia ia: E ka Haku e, ke makemake nei
makou e hai mai oe ia makou i ka inoa a makou e kapa aku ai i
keia ekalesia; no ka mea, aia no na hoopaapaa ana mawaena o
na kanaka no keia mea.
4. A i mai la ka Haku ia lakou: Oiaio, he oiaio ka'u e olelo
aku nei ia oukou, heaha la ka na kanaka mea e ohumu nei a e hoopaapaa nei no keia mea?
5. Aole anei lakou i heluhelu i na palapala hemolele, e olelo
ana, he mea e pono ai no oukou e lawe maluna o oukou i [d] ka
inoa o Kristo, oia no hoi ko'u inoa? No ka mea, ma keia inoa
oukou e kapaia mai ai ma ka la hope;
6. A o ka mea e lawe ana maluna iho ona i ko'u inoa, a e
hoomau ana i ka hopena, oia ke hoolaia ma ka la hope;
7. Nolaila, o kela mea keia mea a oukou e hana'i, e hana
oukou ia mea ma kuu inoa; nolaila, e kapa no oukou i ka ekale-

3 NEPHI, 18

19. Therefore ye must always pray unto the Father in my name;

20. And whatsoever ye shall ask the Father in my name, which is right, believing that ye shall receive, behold it shall be given unto you.

21. [n]Pray in your families unto the Father, always in my name, that your wives and your children may be blessed.

22. And behold, ye shall meet together oft; and ye shall not forbid any man from coming unto you when ye shall meet together, but suffer them that they may come unto you and forbid them not;

23. But ye shall pray for them, and shall not cast them out; and if it so be that they come unto you oft ye shall pray for them unto the Father, in my name.

24. Therefore, hold up your light that it may shine unto the world. Behold I am the [o]light which ye shall hold up—that which ye have seen me do. Behold ye see that I have prayed unto the Father, and ye all have witnessed.

3 NEPHI, 27

CHAPTER 27.

Jesus Christ names his church—All things are written by the Father—Men to be judged by what is written in the books.

1. And it came to pass that as the [a]disciples of Jesus were journeying and were preaching the things which they had both heard and seen, and were baptizing in the name of Jesus, it came to pass that the disciples were gathered together and were united in mighty [b]prayer and [c]fasting.

2. And Jesus again showed himself unto them, for they were praying unto the Father in his name; and Jesus came and stood in the midst of them, and said unto them: What will ye that I shall give unto you?

3. And they said unto him: Lord, we will that thou wouldst tell us the name whereby we shall call this church; for there are disputations among the people concerning this matter.

4. And the Lord said unto them: Verily, verily, I say unto you, why is it that the people should murmur and dispute because of this thing?

5. Have they not read the scriptures, which say ye must take upon you the [d]name of Christ, which is my name? For by this name shall ye be called at the last day;

6. And whoso taketh upon him my name, and endureth to the end, the same shall be saved at the last day.

7. Therefore, whatsoever ye shall do, ye shall do it in my name; therefore ye shall call the church in my name; and ye shall call upon the Father in my name that he will bless the church for my sake.

sia ma ko'u inoa; a e kahea aku oukou i ka Makua ma ko'u inoa, i hoopomaikai mai ai oia i ka ekalesia no'u nei;

8. A pehea la ko'u ekalesia ia, ke kapa ole ia oia ma ko'u inoa? No ka mea, ina e kapaia kekahi ekalesia ma ko Mose inoa, alaila, o ko Mose ekalesia no ia; a, ina e kapaia ia ma ka inoa o kekahi kanaka, alaila, he ekalesia ia no kekahi kanaka; aka, ina e kapaia ia ma ko'u inoa, alaila, o ko'u ekalesia no ia, ina paha i kukuluia oia maluna o ko'u euanelio.

9. He oiaio ka'u e olelo aku nei ia oukou, ua kukuluia oukou maluna o ko'u euanelio; nolaila, e kapa aku oukou i na mea a oukou e kapa aku ai, ma ko'u inoa; nolaila, ina e hea aku oukou i ka Makua, no ka ekalesia, ina ma ko'u inoa ia, alaila, e hoolohe mai no ka Makua i ka oukou;

10. A ina paha i kukuluia ka ekalesia ma ko'u euanelio, alaila, e hoike mai no ka Makua i kana mau hana iho iloko o ka ekalesia;

11. Aka, ina aole ia i kukuluia maluna o ko'u euanelio, a ua kukuluia maluna iho o na hana a kanaka, a i ole ia, maluna iho o na hana o ke diabolo, he oiaio ka'u e olelo aku nei ia oukou, he lealea ka lakou ma ka lakou hana no kekahi manawa, a mahope e hiki mai ana ka hopena, a [e] kuaia lakou ilalo a hooleiia'ku iloko o ke ahi, kahi e hiki ole ai ke hoi mai mailaila mai;

MOKUNA 10.

1. Ano, ke palapala iho nei au, o Moroni, i kekahi mau mea maikai i kuu manao; a ke palapala iho nei au i ko'u poe hoahanau, i ko Lamana poe; a ua makemake au e ike oukou ua hala aku na makahiki eha haneri me ka iwakalua a keu aku, mahope iho o ka haawiia ana mai o ka [a] hoailona no ka hiki ana mai o Kristo.

2. A e sila iho ana au i [b] keia mau mooolelo, mahope iho o ka'u olelo ana i kekahi mau olelo ma ke ano kauleo aku ia oukou.

3. Aia hoi, ke kauleo aku nei au ia oukou, i ka wa a oukou e heluhelu ai i keia mau mea, ina he mea naauao i ke Akua e heluhelu oukou ia mau mea, e hoomanao oukou i ka nani o ko ka Haku aloha ana i na keiki a kanaka, mai ka [c] hanaia'na mai o Adamu, a hiki wale i ka manawa e loaa'i ia oukou keia mau mea, a e noonoo ia mea ma ko oukou mau naau.

4. A ia oukou e loaa'i keia mau mea, ke ake nei au e kauleo aku ia oukou, e ninau aku oukou i ke Akua, i ka Makua mau loa, ma ka inoa o Kristo, ina he oiaio keia mau mea; a ina e ninau aku auanei oukou me ka oiaio o ka naau, me ka makemake io, me ka manaoio ia Kristo, nana no e hoike mai i ka oiaio o ia mea ia oukou, [d] ma ka mana o ka Uhane Hemolele;

5. A ma ka mana o ka Uhane Hemolele, ua hiki ia oukou ke ike i ka oiaio o na mea a pau.

3 NEPHI, 27

8. And how be it my church
save it be called in my name?
For if a church be called in
Moses' name then it be Moses'
church; or if it be called in the
name of a man then it be the
church of a man; but if it be
called in my name then it is my
church, if it so be that they are
built upon my gospel.
9. Verily I say unto you, that
ye are built upon my gospel;
therefore ye shall call whatsoever
things ye do call, in my name;
therefore if ye call upon the Father, for the church, if it be in
my name the Father will hear
you;
10. And if it so be that the
church is built upon my gospel
then will the Father show forth
his own works in it.
11. But if it be not built upon
my gospel, and is built upon the
works of men, or upon the works
of the devil, verily I say unto you
they have joy in their works for
a season, and by and by the end
cometh, and they are [e]hewn
down and cast into the fire, from
whence there is no return.

MORONI, 10

CHAPTER 10.

Moroni's farewell to the Lamanites—Conditions on which individual testimony of the truth of the Book of Mormon may be obtained—Moroni seals up the record of his people.

1. Now I, Moroni, write somewhat as seemeth me good; and I
write unto my brethren, the Lamanites; and I would that they
should know that *more than
four hundred and twenty years
have passed away since the [a]sign
was given of the coming of Christ.
2. And I seal up [b]these records,
after I have spoken a few words
by way of exhortation unto you.
3. Behold, I would exhort you
that when ye shall read these
things, if it be wisdom in God that
ye should read them, that ye
would remember how merciful
the Lord hath been unto the children of men, from the [c]creation
of Adam even down unto the time
that ye shall receive these things,
and ponder it in your hearts.
4. And when ye shall receive
these things, I would exhort you
that ye would ask God, the Eternal Father, in the name of Christ,
if these things are not true; and
if ye shall ask with a sincere
heart, with real intent, having
faith in Christ, he will manifest
the truth of it unto you, [d]by the
power of the Holy Ghost.
5. And by the power of the
Holy Ghost ye may know the
truth of all things.

6. A o kela mea keia mea i maikai, ua pololei a oiaio hoi;
nolaila, aohe mea i maikai e hoole ana i ke Kristo, aka, e hooia
ana ke ola la oia.
7. A ua hiki ia oukou ke ike ke ola la oia, ma ka mana o ka
Uhane Hemolele; nolaila, ke ake nei au e ao ikaika aku ia oukou,
i ole ai oukou e [e]hoole aku i ka mana o ke Akua; no ka mea, e
hana ana oia ma o ka mana la, e [f]like me ka manaoio o na keiki
a kanaka, [g]oia like i keia la, i ka la apopo, a no ka wa pau ole.
8. A ke ao ikaika hou aku nei au ia oukou, e ko'u poe hoahanau, i ole ai oukou e [h]hoole aku i na haawina o ke Akua, no
ka mea, he nui ia mau mea; a ke hele mai nei ia mau mea mai
ia Akua hookahi mai. A he nui na ano o ka lawelaweia ana
o keia mau haawina; aka, o ke Akua hookahi nana e hana nei i na
mea a pau; a ua haawiia mai ia mau mea ma na hoikeana o ka
Uhane o ke Akua i na kanaka i mea e pono ai lakou.
9. [i]No ka mea, aia, ua haawiia mai i kekahi ma ka Uhane o
ke Akua, i ao aku ai oia i ka olelo o ka naauao;
10. A i kekahi, i ao aku ai oia i ka olelo o ka ike ma ka Uhane
hookahi no;
11. A i kekahi, ka manaoio nui loa; a i kekahi, na haawina
o ka hoola ana ma ka Uhane hookahi no.
12. A i kekahi hoi, i hana aku ai oia i na hana mana nui;
13. A i kekahi hoi, i wanana aku ai oia no na mea a pau;
14. A i kekahi hoi, ka ike ana i na anela a me na uhane lawelawe;
15. A i kekahi hoi, na ano a pau o na olelo;
16. A i kekahi hoi, ka hoomaopopo ana i na olelo a me kela
ano keia ano o na olelo.
17. A e hiki mai keia mau haawina a pau ma o ka Uhane la
o Kristo; a e hiki mai keia mau mea i kela kanaka keia kanaka
pakahi, e like me ia i makemake ai.
18. A ke ake nei au e ao ikaika aku ia oukou, e ko'u poe hoahanau aloha, e hoomanao oukou e hiki mai ana [j]kela haawina
maikai keia haawina maikai no Kristo mai.
19. A ke ake nei au e ao ikaika aku ia oukou, e kuu poe hoahanau i alohaia, e hoomanao oukou [k]oia like no ia, inehinei, i
keia la, a no ka wa pau ole, a, [l]aole loa e hoopauia aku keia
mau haawina a pau a'u i olelo aku ai, no ko ka Uhane ia mau
mea, a mau loa aku, oiai e ku ana ke ao nei, aka mamuli o ka
hoomaloka o na keiki a kanaka wale no e pau ai.
20. Nolaila, [m]he manaoio e pono ai; a ina he manaoio e pono
ai, alaila, he manaolana no hoi e pono ai; a ina he manaolana e
pono ai, alaila, he aloha no hoi e pono ai;
21. A ke ole he aloha ko oukou, aole loa e hiki ke hoolaia oukou ma ke aupuni o ke Akua; aohe no hoi e hiki ke hoolaia oukou
ma ke aupuni o ke Akua, ina he manaoio ole ko oukou; aole no
hoi e hiki oukou ina aole he manaolana ko oukou;

6. And whatsoever thing is good is just and true; wherefore, nothing that is good denieth the Christ, but acknowledgeth that he is.

7. And ye may know that he is, by the power of the Holy Ghost; wherefore I would exhort you that ye deny [e]not the power of God; for he worketh by power, [f]according to the faith of the children of men, the [g]same today and tomorrow, and forever.

8. And again, I exhort you, my brethren, that ye [h]deny not the gifts of God, for they are many; and they come from the same God. And there are different ways that these gifts are administered; but it is the same God who worketh all in all; and they are given by the manifestations of the Spirit of God unto men, to profit them.

9. [i]For behold, to one is given by the Spirit of God, that he may teach the word of wisdom;

10. And to another, that he may teach the word of knowledge by the same Spirit;

11. And to another, exceeding great faith; and to another, the gifts of healing by the same Spirit;

12. And again, to another, that he may work mighty miracles;

13. And again, to another, that he may prophesy concerning all things;

14. And again, to another, the beholding of angels and ministering spirits;

15. And again, to another, all kinds of tongues;

16. And again, to another, the interpretation of languages and of divers kinds of tongues.

17. And all these gifts come by the Spirit of Christ; and they come unto every man severally, according as he will.

18. And I would exhort you, my beloved brethren, that ye remember that [j]every good gift cometh of Christ.

19. And I would exhort you, my beloved brethren, that ye remember that he is the [k]same yesterday, today, and forever, and that all these gifts of which I have spoken, which are spiritual, [l]never will be done away, even as long as the world shall stand, only according to the unbelief of the children of men.

20. [m]Wherefore, there must be faith; and if there must be faith there must also be hope; and if there must be hope there must also be charity.

21. And except ye have charity ye can in nowise be saved in the kingdom of God; neither can ye be saved in the kingdom of God if ye have not faith; neither can ye if ye have no hope.

22. A ina aole o oukou manaolana, alaila ua poho loa ko oukou manao; a e hiki ana ka poho loa o ka manao no ka hewa.

23. A olelo oiaio mai la o Kristo i ko kakou poe kupuna, [n]Ina he manaoio ko oukou, ua hiki ia oukou ke hana i na mea a pau i ku pono ia'u.

24. Ano, ke olelo aku nei au i ko na welau a pau o ka honua, [o]ina e hiki mai ka la e hoopauia'i ka mana a me na haawina o ke Akua mawaena o oukou, e hanaia auanei ia mea mamuli o ka hoomaloka.

25. A auwe na keiki a kanaka, ina pela ia auanei; no ka mea, aole kekahi mea e hana ana i ka pono mawaena o oukou, aole loa hookahi. No ka mea, ina e hana ana kekahi i ka pono mawaena o oukou, e hana no oia ma ka mana a me na haawina o ke Akua.

26. A auwe ka poe nana e hoopau ae i keia mau mea a make, no ka mea, e make ana lakou iloko o ko lakou mau hewa, a ua hiki ole ke hoolaia lakou ma ke aupuni o ke Akua; a ke olelo aku nei au ia mea mamuli o na olelo a Kristo, aole o'u wahahee.

27. A ke ao ikaika nei au ia oukou e hoomanao iho i keia mau mea; no ka mea, e [p]hiki koke mai ana ka manawa e ike ai oukou aole o'u wahahee, no ka mea, e ike auanei oukou ia'u ma kahi hookolokolo o ke Akua, a e olelo aku ka Haku ke Akua ia oukou, Aole anei au i hai aku i ka'u mau olelo ia oukou, i na mea i palapalaia e keia kanaka, e like me kekahi e [q]hea ana mai ka lepo ae; he oiaio, e like me kekahi e olelo ana noloko mai o ka lepo?

28. Ke hai aku nei au i keia mau mea i ka hookoia ana o na wanana. A, aia hoi, e puka mai ia mau mea noloko mai o ka waha o ke Akua mau loa; a [r]e ha ae kana olelo ia hanauna aku ia hanauna aku.

29. A e [s]hoike ae no ke Akua ia oukou, o ka mea a'u i palapala ai, he oiaio.

30. A eia hou, ke makemake nei au e ao ikaika ia oukou, e hele mai oukou io Kristo la, a e hopu i kela [t]haawina maikai i keia haawina maikai, a e [u]hoopa ole i ka haawina ino, aohe hoi i ka mea haumia.

31. A e ala, a [v]e ea ae mai ka lepo ae, e Ierusalema; he oiaio, a e komo i kou lole nani, e ke kaikamahine o Ziona, a e hooikaika i kou mau kakia, a e hooakea aku i kou mau mokuna no ka wa pau ole, i [w]hoohoka hou ole ia'i oe, i [x]hookoia'i na berita a ka Makua mau loa i hana mai ai ia oe, e ko ka hale o Iseraela.

22. And if ye have no hope ye
must needs be in despair; and
despair cometh because of iniquity.
23. And Christ truly said unto
our fathers: [n]If ye have faith ye
can do all things which are expedient unto me.
24. And now I speak unto all
the ends of the earth—[o]that if
the day cometh that the power
and gifts of God shall be done
away among you, it shall be because of unbelief.
25. And wo be unto the children of men if this be the case;
for there shall be none that doeth
good among you, no not one.
For if there be one among you
that doeth good, he shall work
by the power and gifts of God.
26. And wo unto them who
shall do these things away and
die, for they die in their sins, and
they cannot be saved in the kingdom of God; and I speak it according to the words of Christ;
and I lie not.
27. And I exhort you to remember these things; for the
time speedily cometh that ye
shall [p]know that I lie not. for ye
shall see me at the bar of God;
and the Lord God will say unto
you: Did I not declare my words
unto you, which were written
by this man, like as one [q]crying
from the dead, yea, even as one
speaking out of the dust?
28. I declare these things unto
the fulfilling of the prophecies.
And behold, they shall proceed
forth out of the mouth of the
everlasting God; and his word
shall [r]hiss forth from generation
to generation.
29. And God shall [s]show unto
you, that that which I have
written is true.
30. And again I would exhort
you that ye would come unto
Christ, and lay hold upon every
[t]good gift, and [u]touch not the
evil gift, nor the unclean thing.
31. And awake, and [v]arise from
the dust, O Jerusalem; yea, and
put on thy beautiful garments, O
daughter of Zion; and strengthen
thy stakes and enlarge thy borders forever, that thou mayest
[w]no more be confounded, that the
[x]covenants of the Eternal Father
which he hath made unto thee, O
house of Israel, may be fulfilled.

32. He oiaio, e hele mai io Kristo la, a e hoohemoleleia iloko ona, a e hoole ia oukou iho i na mea hewa a pau; a ina e hoole ia oukou iho i na mea hewa a pau, a e aloha aku i ke Akua me ko oukou mana, naau, a ikaika a pau, alaila, ua lawa kona lokomaikai no oukou, i hemolele ai oukou ma o kona lokomaikai la iloko o Kristo; a ina ma ka lokomaikai o ke Akua ua hemolele oukou iloko o Kristo, ua hiki ole ia oukou ma kekahi mea, ke [v]hoole i ka mana o ke Akua.

33. A eia hou, ina hemolele oukou iloko o Kristo, ma o ka lokomaikai la o ke Akua, aole hoi hoole i kona mana, alaila ua hoomaemaeia oukou iloko o Kristo ma ka lokomaikai o ke Akua, ma o ka [z]hookaheia'na la o ke koko o Kristo, oia no ka berita a ka Makua i ke kalaia'na o ko oukou mau hala, i lilo ai oukou i hemolele me ke kina ole.

34. Ano, ke uwe aloha aku nei au ia oukou a pau. E hele koke ana au e maha ma ka [2a]paradaiso o ke Akua, a hiki wale i ka wa e [2b]hui pu hou ai kuu uhane a me kuu kino, a lawe lanakila ia aku au maloko aku o ka lewa, e halawai pu me oukou [2c]imua o kahi hookolokolo oluolu o Iehova ka nui, ka Lunakanawai mau loa o ka poe ola a me ka poe make. Amene.

32. Yea, come unto Christ, and be perfected in him, and deny yourselves of all ungodliness; and if ye shall deny yourselves of all ungodliness and love God with all your might, mind and strength, then is his grace sufficient for you, that by his grace ye may be perfect in Christ; and if by the grace of God ye are perfect in Christ, ye can in [y]nowise deny the power of God.

33. And again, if ye by the grace of God are perfect in Christ, and deny not his power, then are ye sanctified in Christ by the grace of God, through the [z]shedding of the blood of Christ, which is in the covenant of the Father unto the remission of your sins, that ye become holy, without spot.

34. And now I bid unto all, farewell. I soon go to rest in the [2a]paradise of God, until my spirit and body shall again [2b]reunite, and I am brought forth triumphant through the air, to meet you before the [2c]pleasing bar of the great Jehovah, the Eternal Judge of both quick and dead. Amen.